# Portraits From the Beginnings

# Portraits From the Beginnings

## They Walked With God

# SANNA BARLOW ROSSI

**To order additional copies of this book, contact:**
Xlibris Corporation
1-888-795-4274
www.Xlibris.com
Orders@Xlibris.com
24729

# Contents

To the
Bradenton Missionary Village
whose lives and ministry bless us all
this book is dedicated.

# Acknowledgments

My sincere thanks to Betty Coleman for her skill and diligence in the hours of work as she helped me with the computer, and is responsible for getting this contemplation into manuscript.

# Foreword

ew Christians have diligently studied the lives of the Patriarchs, as revealed in the book of Genesis, as the author of this study. Brought up in the home of a mother, in whom God placed a special gift of teaching His Word, the author early developed a love for God and His word.

As a young person, she pursued the learning of the Bible during the depression years at Columbia Bible College. Because of her love of God's Word, she became a missionary traveling across the globe seeking to insure that as many Bibleless people as possible would have some portion of her precious Bible in their heart language.

Who could predict that in her later years, she would be married to one of the great entrepreneurs of the United States. She shared in loving concern with him, much of God's grace showered upon a host of God's people.

Throughout two decades, she pursued a deeper understanding of the book of Genesis' presentation of the Patriarchs of God. In this volume, she shares some of the personal things she has learned. As you read "Portraits from The Beginnings, They Walked with God", You will be exposed to the heart of a sensitive and close follower of her Savior, the Lord Jesus Christ, and be drawn closer to the God of eternity.

John E. Kyle

# Introduction

"*I* remember, when a child, looking intently into the glorious blue of the sky with its moving, shaping, re-shaping clouds, and wishing I could see God, could talk to Him, know Him. What is He like? My probing wonder could not begin to grasp the Eternal Being who made those clouds and the heaven above.

The Book given us by the Eternal God, which we call The Holy Bible, opens with these words: "In the beginning God," God is already there. (Genesis 1:1)

Once a six-year-old asked me, "Teacher, who made God?" His blue eyes were eager and bright, a freckled face tow-head, live-wire little boy. I answered with another question:

"What do you think?"

"Well, I think He made Hisself, I reckon." Then he thought more deeply: "I guess He'd been thinking about it a long time, I reckon."

How could this alert first-grader handle my answer, "God has always been. Before He made anything, He was there already."?

Contemplating the mystery of the eternal transcendent God, outside of time and space, brings with it a keen sense of loneliness, smallness, and awe that are a kind of fear. Yet it is this very awe of God, this reverence, this fear that the Bible often states "is the beginning of wisdom."

As the book of Genesis opens, "In the beginning God created the heavens and the earth," the far-off eternal One draws nearer. He made the earth where we live. And on this earth He contemplates the creation of man and woman. It is George MacDonald who points out the great truth of God's immanence in His creation on planet earth. He says:

"Of all teaching that which presents a far distant God is the nearest to absurdity. Either there is none, or He is nearer to every one of us than our nearest consciousness of self." (from "George MacDonald, An Anthology" by C S Lewis. London Geoffrey Bles, page 116 # 321)

In the second chapter of Genesis, God said, "Let us make man in our own image.' The word, God, here is the plural "Elohim," suggesting the triune nature of God.

A few paragraphs into the Genesis account, some startling words tell us of the Lord God Himself talking with the first man and woman whom He had made of the dust of the earth! For He made them more than mortal bodies, *but living souls*. He had breathed into them the breath of life, the Life that was of Himself, everlasting in its essence.

This God did so that Man would have the capability of knowing Him. Thus He built into Man's soul an innate need for God. This is why a person's supreme fulfillment and joy are found in communion with his Maker.

Have you ever wondered what God taught the first man and woman in His daily trysts with them? What did His own, and best of all His Creation ask Him then? For it must have been from Adam that Job had learned the incredible truths of Creation and the laws of Nature recorded in his book, the most ancient of the scriptures.Who taught him of the stars and the constellations with their names? Who revealed to

Adam the character and many of the attributes of God Himself? Who put understanding in the mind of man? How could Adam have understood enough about the animal creation to name them all significantly? In the book of the prophet Isaiah, we find him commenting on man's understanding of how to plough and sow and harvest wheat barley and other grains; also of his judgment in knowing how to process it into flour. And Isaiah says,

"For He instructs him in the right judgment, His God teaches him . . . This also comes from the Lord of hosts who is wonderful in counsel and excellent in guidance." (Isaiah 28:26,29)

We do not know how long a time period this order of man's ways continued in his perfect environment in Eden. But we can discern that Adam and Eve were created to know and to enjoy God, and in so doing to glorify Him. Reflecting His likeness glorifies God.

It is this fact which explains why the human spirit cannot be satisfied or realize lasting joy until it finds Him in that bondage to His love which becomes our best motive for obedience to Him and is, therefore, our truest liberty and rest.

Further on in Genesis chapter two we find that God, in a mode appropriate to their human limitations, habitually walked with Adam and Eve in the garden. The Lord Himself delighted in His crowning creation, made in His likeness in their mental, moral, and spiritual essential being.

Even though God's perfect plan was ruined by the sin factor entering into the heart of God's beloved people, He did not allow His eternal purposes in love to fail.

Tragic as the consequences of sin would prove to be, it is overwhelming to observe that:

"If we take history as a whole, watching the movement of the centuries, we see the purposes of the

Almighty marching down the ages with irresistable tread, and pushing on to that 'one far off event to which the whole creation moves,'" (Sidlow Baxter, God So Loved page 29)

That Event is the pivotal event of human history, the Incarnation, when the calendar changes from BC to AD.

From the very beginning we can note God's dealing with individuals is personal, intimate, near. The Almighty Himself is walking through these pages of scripture, immanent within His Creation, intercepting time on earth to write its other story of a new Creation with a permanence that the Eternal alone can effect. God is constantly beseeching those who will respond to Him to become a part of His own inheritance and forever to walk with Him. It is in the importance of this truth that *we* choose to live today in fellowship with God. He can actually become the Home of our inner being, of our thoughts and motives. So that even as the years move swiftly by, we may experience the blessing Paul speaks of when he says,

"Therefore we do not lose heart. Even though our outward man is perishing, our inward man is *being renewed day by day."* (2 Cor. 4:16)

For this reason, the Portraits of eight persons who lived in the time scope of Genesis, may inspire us in their experience of faith, their revelation of God, and consequent knowledge of Him.

*For they walked with God.*

# Night and Day

Into the black depths of empty space
When Time began, God spoke "Let there be light".
A rush of stars appeared in every place
A host of lanterns lit upon the night

For God had made the darkness to give way
To speeding orbs aflame we see today.

Upon earth's surface turning from the night
God showed the dawn her glowing start.
As sunrise flooded half the world with light
The morning was the evening's counterpart.

And there was evening and morning, night and day.
And God declared them good,
Whom stars and sun obey.

# Chapter One

## What is Man?

"By Creation, we have the capacity
to know God." (A W Tozer)

The story of mankind began in a garden called Delight. The Garden of Eden. Adam, with Eve, the summit of God's creation, was yet human and frail against the vast wonder of God's handiwork, the heavens and the earth.

Should we not then marvel with the Psalmist, lift up our eyes to the Eternal and ask,

"What is man that You are mindful of him?"

"When I consider Your heavens, the work of Your fingers, the moon and the stars which You have ordained. Why man? And" "Who is he that You are mindful of him, . . . that You visit him?" (Psalm 8:3,4)

For Adam was not born; God made him with His own creative initiative. He "breathed into him the breath of life, and man became a living being" (Genesis 2:7)

He was clothed in a body suited for life on earth, but this was only his exterior self. Far more important is the marvelous fact that God had set "eternity in his heart", (Ecc. 3:10) and created Adam and Eve in His own likeness.

This likeness was not only man's moral uprightness reflecting God, but his inbuilt *capacity* to *know God*. Adam and Eve were also spirit, a wondrous component given to them by God who is the Eternal Spirit, "the Father of spirits", (Heb. 12:9) so that they could partake of the very life of God!

*God created them to walk with Him.*

They were immortal souls that would not dissolve in dust and ashes as their temporary dress must do, for their immortal being must outlast Time.

God had placed Adam and Eve in Eden to enjoy and tend the garden, To till it was God's gift of purposeful activity to bring to each new day the joy of creative accomplishment.

Adam was to have "dominion over the fish of the sea, over the birds of the air, and over every living thing that moves in the earth," (Genesis 1:28)

The Psalmist, still pondering this mystery, exclaims again, "What is man? have made him a little lower than the angels, and You have crowned him with glory and honor, . . . You have put everything under his feet." (Psalm 8:6)

If we marvel today at the breath-taking beauties of planet earth, how much more perfect it must have been when newly spoken into being by the Eternal Word of Elohim: God who is Father, Word, and Holy Spirit?

"In the beginning was the Word, and the Word was with God, and the Word was God. All things were made by Him, and without Him, nothing was made that was made. In Him was life, and the life was the light of man". (John 1:1-4)

Creation began when God spoke light out of darkness. He brought into a formless void the light of day with each day's night brilliant with the myriad galaxies of the heavens, the moon and the stars to declare the glory of God.

The poem of Creation, in Genesis chapter one, tells

of the six days in which God spoke all things into being and called them good.

Yet the question persists: What is Man? Why?

Amid all the multiplied blessings of Eden to delight Adam and Eve, God Himself entered their Garden to walk and talk with them day by day. Daily they anticipated "the voice of God walking in the garden". Here is the Word, God Himself, expressed in terms Adam and Eve could relate to. Designed to fellowship with their Maker, they found in His company the crowning pleasure of each ending day. The Lord had become their Divine Companion, their central joy, their reason for being. Hence, the joy of their Lord pervaded all else in life with happiness ordained of God for His children. For God is the Author of happiness and joy!

"He is our Source, our Center, and our Dwelling-place" wrote Madame de la Motte—Guyon, (From A W Tozer, "The Christian Book of Mystic Verse" p 65)

Again, we may ponder about that time space in which Adam walked in innocence with his Maker . . . What did God tell them?

Who taught Job about the circle of the earth, how it "hangs upon nothing"? We are looking at the Beginnings here; not the Middle Ages of human history. They knew the earth was round, not flat! How did he understand that it was the Almighty Who gave man wide knowledge, and wisdom? Who made man upright and taught him right from wrong? Who gave man the gift of language?

"Who teaches like Him?" (Job 36:22)

The question, "What is Man?" was prayerfully studied by the godly men who composed the Westminster Catechism which begins with "What is the chief end of man?" They state the answer, "Man's chief end is to glorify God and enjoy Him forever."

In writing of this statement. C S Lewis, points out that to "fully enjoy God is to glorify Him. In commanding us to glorify Him, God is inviting us to enjoy Him." (From Reflections on the Psalms, chapter 9)

It is clear that God made us with a need for Himself. We were created to enjoy God. Our inmost being will be satisfied with nothing less than God Himself. When this is a reality for us, we are enabled to glorify Him as His reflection can be mirrored in our attitudes, our goals, our everyday living for others, which tokens His life in us.

A W Tozer in commenting on the words of Bernard of Cluny, of the twelfth century, writes,

"Here we find the triumphal answer to that question about the chief end of man, and so do all who read sympathetically his lovely and inspired poem, "The Celestial Country"

> Exult, O dust and ashes,
> The Lord shall be thy part,
> His only, His forever,
> Thou shalt be, and thou art.

(from The Christian Book of Mystic Verse", A W Tozer p 140, Christian Publications, Camp Hill, Pa.)

A benediction for this meditation comes from Bernard of Clairvaux (1091-1158) in his hymn, "O Jesus Most Wonderful".

> Thee may our hearts forever bless,
> Thee may we love alone;
> And ever in our lives express
> The image of Thine own.

(from "The Christian Book of Christian Verse, A W Tozer, p 95)

The truth at the very core of our existence then, is that we are created for God, to walk with Him in our earthly robe, to walk with Him even as this mortal has been "further clothed" for heaven and swallowed up by Life. (2 Cor. 5:4)

The historical documentation of Genesis repeats often the exciting phrase, he "walked with God." That tells us man's life-line to Him has never ceased. Nevertheless man's ideal environment does change, and the ageless conflict between righteousness and evil begins on earth. God's plans for mankind are challenged. Yet, forever "He is not willing that any should perish." (2 Peter 3:9)

## Perfections of Praise

Let everything with breath declare
Perfections of Thy praise,
For Thou art present everywhere
And wonderful, Thy ways.

I find a tiny flower star
Low hiding in the grass.
And in a bed where roses are
The dewdrops shine like glass.

I hear Thee whisper in the trees,
From feathered folk, Thy song.
I feel Thy Breath upon the breeze,
Thy mercies all day long.

In Thy minute and diverse things
I know that Thou art near,
In patterns of a butterfly wings,
Thy gladsome touch is clear.

Thy multitude of mercies small
Invite me to enjoy,
And see thy caring best of all
In Thy fulfilling joy.

For Thou art present everywhere
And wonderful Thy ways.
Let everything with breath declare
Perfections of Thy praise.

# Chapter Two

## Eden Lost

"Do not cast me away from Thy
presence." (Psalm 51:11)

One can imagine how morning wakened upon
Eden with symphonious birdsong in a
major key, the chatter of glad creatures, the
fragrance of flowers in bloom, and ripening fruit. Best
of all, this was the Garden of the Lord.

Adam and Eve sensed His presence in the soft mist
shimmering in the light of the newly risen sun. They
remembered many trysts with God, and kept on
hearing His voice,

"I have called you by name, you are mine." (Isaiah 43:1)

Instinctively they knew what we who love Him also
understand.

"He meant us to see Him, live with Him and draw
our lives from His smile." (Tozer: The Pursuit of God)

Augustine has wonderfully stated the "origin and
interior history of the human race,"

"Thou hast formed us for Thyself, and our hearts
are restless till they rest in thee." (A.W. Tozer: The
Pursuit of God)

Adam and Eve anticipated more today than just His
footprints in the garden. They would hear His voice in
the cool of the evening, His counseling, and delightful
company in hushed and joyful peace.

"O marvelous! O wonderful
No song or sound is heard
But everywhere and every hour
In love, in wisdom and in power
The Father speaks His dear Eternal Word."
(F.W. Faber: "The Eternal Father")

A.W. Tozer describes the voice of God in his "Pursuit of God":

"God is forever seeking to speak Himself out to His creation. God is speaking. He is, by His nature, continually articulate. He fills the world with His speaking voice."

"That voice which antedates the Bible by uncounted centuries, that voice that has not been silent since the dawn of creation, but is sounding still throughout the full far reaches of the universe."

God is present also in minutest things. The star flower in the grass is tiny but its perfection speaks His touch.

Adam, amid the foliage pruning, worked with a singing heart. Nature yielded gladly to his labor. God was there in all the trivia of daily tasks.

Adam and Eve lived in harmony with each other and with God. He had given them an intensive moral likeness to Himself.

"Our mental and moral nature is made in the same plane as God's: The divine in miniature." (F.B. Meyer: "The Way Into the Holiest")

However, in creating people, God did not make them to be robots. Like Himself in personhood, they could exercise freedom of will. God did not design our doing His will because we *must*, but rather by our *own deliberate choice*. We could decide to love Him best, not for His blessings but for Himself; or we could choose to please ourselves, seeking a liberty that would prove itself a bitter bondage in the end.

"There is a way that seems right to a man, but its end is the way of death." (Proverbs 14:12)

"Do not eat of the Tree in the midst of the Garden," God had commanded. He also gave the reason for His command:

"For in the day that you eat thereof, you shall surely die."

It was the knowledge of good and evil. God made known His will clearly with His warning to safeguard His beloved creation from utmost harm.

This tree, solitary among all the other trees whose fruit they could enjoy, was God's test to prove whether His own created being would choose to obey Him or not.

One day in Eden, Eve passed by that forbidden tree, and she saw a beautiful creature standing by the tree, the Serpent which was the most attractive of all the creatures God had made. But this one was disguising the evil Antagonist of God. Once a cherub of glorious mien, in pride he had rebelled against God, and against goodness, to become the Dark Antithesis to God, and to His attributes of love, holiness, mercy and truth.

Eve paused to talk with the Serpent who embodied the spirit of Satan, as he pointed out to her the desirable fruit ripened in its branches. When the Serpent offered the fruit to Eve, she correctly rejected his proffer:

"The Lord said, 'You shall not eat of it. In the day you eat it, you will surely die'" (Gen. 3:3)

At this moment, Eve was quoting God's Word. She was right to have aligned herself with it in resisting the tempter.

Millenniums after this early hour of human history, the One who is Adam II, confronted the Tempter as Eve did, only He was in a desert, not a garden, after forty days of fasting there. Approached along the same three avenues by which we likewise can be drawn into sin, He resisted Satan by using the Word of God. Like a sword, His "It is written you shall not", foiled the attempt of the Evil one every time. (Matthew 4:10)

"Resist the devil and he will flee from you." was proved true, as is also the axiom, "Draw near to God and he will draw near to you." (James 4:7,8)

"Then the angels ministered unto Him." (Matt. 4:11)

He was the incarnate Word. However, in the resources given to all of us, Jesus of Nazareth overcame temptation "such as is common to man" *by God's Word alone*: (I Cor. 10:13)


"It is written, 'Man shall not live by bread alone, but by every word that proceeds from the mouth of God.'" (Matt. 4:4)

The simplicity of victory over Satan is to make God's will my will. Obedience is the fruit of saying "Yes" to God.

Back in Eden, the soft smooth voice of the Serpent began to cast doubt on God, His motives, His credibility, His character. Considering the deceiver's argument, Eve began to think about the fruit of the Tree of the Knowledge of Good and Evil. And at every one of the three points of vulnerability, "the lust of the flesh, the lust of the eyes, the pride of life", she chose to please herself. Doubting God, it was easy to disobey. She partook of the fruit.

Immediately a darkness fell upon Eve's soul once alight with the life of God. She had tasted evil, and learned the guilt of sin.

"Obedience is the high calling of life in Christ, and implicit in it is a daily death to the self-life that clamors for its own." (a quotation in a letter from Eileen Kuhn).

When Adam found Eve, trembling and ashamed, and saw the sneer on the Serpent's face, he knew what had just happened. Would he now join his wife, bone of his bone, flesh of his flesh, or would he cling to God?

With his eyes open, Adam took the fruit Eve gave him, and disobeyed the Lord. Both were frightened and guilty so they hid among the trees of the garden when they heard the voice of God calling,

*"Adam, Adam where are you?"*

The pathos in that voice would be echoed down through the ages until the Lord Himself became the incarnate "Man of sorrows and acquainted with grief." (Isaiah 53:3)

Spiritual death which is separation from God, must be addressed and reversed.Before time began, the eternal decree had been established, that the Lamb of God would take away the sins of the world. On another Tree, the Cross, He would bear our sins in His own body. (I Peter 2:24) That body would be the Seed of the Woman, the Seed of Abraham, the Word made flesh.

In a timespan of thirty-three years, the Lord God of Eden, now the son of man, would walk on earth among men to finish that work the ancient altar signified. He would accomplish this by His death on the cross, planted on a hill called Golgotha, the place of the skull, where the Savior accomplished the atonement for sin. He fully paid forever "the wages of sin" which is death, to offer to everyone who trusts Him, "the gift of God which is eternal life." (Romans 3:23)

Risen from death, the Eternal Son saves to the uttermost "all those who come to God by him." (Heb. 9:25)

The shadow of death had fallen upon Eden when Adam and Eve stood guilty before God in that early hour of time. They heard Him speak the severe words of judgment upon sin: toil and pain and eventual death would replace that garden, "a heaven upon earth."

Banished from Eden where the cherubim at the east of the garden brandished a flaming sword, Adam and Eve in an alien setting, turned to "till the ground from which they had been taken." (Genesis 3:23)

God had spoken in the severity of His justice, first to the Evil One within the Serpent, then to Eve, and last, to Adam. Judgment spelled out sorrow, pain and toil with its thorns and thistles, and finally, human mortality:

"For dust you are and to dust you shall return." (Genesis 3:19)

Yet all was not black. In judgment God remembered mercy. God gave Adam and Eve the *hope* that would enlighten all of the oncoming years and generations. He had not forgotten man's everlasting part, His soul's immortality. And though sin had separated his spiritual being from communion with a Holy God, God brought to him the *immediate* cure: In the meaning of the altar and its sin-offering, God could, right then, forgive all sin and restore him to *keep on walking with God.*

"The path across the gulf that divides right from wrong is not the fire, but repentance." (George MacDonald "Discovering the Character of God" p 259, by Michael Phillips, Bethany House Publishers)

In the mind of God, the work of man's redemption was already "Truth that endures unto all generations." (Psalm:100:5)

The atonement for sin which the Eternal Word fulfilled in His ordained time in history was effective immediately for the individual who, in his own day, trusted God, beginning at the altar which fore-shadowed the atonement. This means of our salvation was indelibly written in "the determinate council and foreknowledge of God."

God addressed His adversary, the Serpent and said:

"And I will put enmity
between you and the woman
And between your seed and her Seed,
He shall bruise your head
And you shall bruise his heel." (Genesis 3:15)

As the eternal Maker of the Universe spoke these words, He Himself felt that bruised heel. At what cost would our "mighty Maker die, for man, the creature's sin?"! (Hymn: "Alas, And Did My Savior Bleed" by Isaac Watts, stanza three.)

The Eternal Himself has suffered with us and for us in the redeeming miracle of the cross." (Sidlow Baxter in "God So Loved")

The conflict of the ages entered into human history at its beginning. But divine conquest, throughout the generations of man would yet secure the glory and over-ruling Kingdom of God. And all God's children of Adam who have chosen to trust and obey Him, shall once more be among God's own in what Christ calls "the age to come". (Luke 18:29,30)

"For God so loved the world that He gave His only begotten Son that *whoever* believes in Him should not perish but have everlasting life." (John 3:16)

When he stood before God at the altar and its sacrifice, Adam trusted and worshiped God. Access to God was restored to him and to all his race.

As the years of time lengthened, there were always some who looked to God and trusted in Him—a great number no doubt (the Genesis record is too brief to mention them) who knew God, and each in his own generation *chose to walk with Him.*

It was by these that God shaped a new creation to

forever live in His presence in transforming "newness of life." (Romans 6:4)

Adam's second son, Abel, was the first of those whose faith would be a lighted window upon the smile of God.

# Thy Presence Here

Beloved, in the cool of evening
Vespers of the ending day,
I can hear Thy footsteps nearing
To walk with me, and with me stay.

Music of my Shepherd's voice,
Large and mighty, small and dear,
Lifts my spirit to rejoice,
So gladsome is Thy Presence here.

Nearer to Thine own than breathing.
Closer Thou than hands and feet,
To my soul, Thyself bequeathing,
Thou hast made my life complete.

Savior-Shepherd of the sheep,
Make Thine own to walk with Thee.
Thy voice to know, Thy word to keep
Now and for eternity.

Beloved, as the day is fading
And watchers of the night do shine,
Whispers in the trees pervading
Sing of Thee that Thou art mine.

# Chapter Three

## The Faith of Abel

"Atonement is provided for iniquity." Prov. 16:6

Human history had begun in a Paradise where man and woman walked with God in perfect fellowship, heart to heart. Clothed in light, they walked in the purity of innocence and spiritual compatibility, inwardly centered in the One who made them for Himself.

But now, Adam and Eve lived outside Eden. The exact geographic locality is not stated in the Genesis record (Gen. 4:1-16). Yet, in careful reading of their lives in this place, it is clear that they were still very much in touch with God. They were aware of the present God.

When Cain, Eve's first born, is named she exclaimed, "I have gotten a man from the Lord!" In her words is the strong inference,

"Could this one be that promised One to crush the Serpent's head?".

After Cain, his brother Abel was born. We may imagine the hours, and days and years that followed, filled with little joys and delights that our Maker has blessed His beloved creation with, "His multitude of mercies" that indicate God's enduring loving-kindness. In these is His tender touch and the sense that "the everyday-ness of life is penetrated by glory." (C. S. Lewis)

There was the golden entry of each new day, the glad energy of living, the diversity of all God's bounty, and "daily bread", the work ethic, as well, with the special gratification of purpose and achievement. Though life was not easy as it had been in Eden, Cain labored, tilling the ground, and one day brought an offering to the Lord of its choicest fruit. As youths, both Cain and Abel recognized God, their Maker, Source of life and blessing. Abel also brought his offering "the firstlings of his flock, and their fat." God was there to meet with both the givers and their gifts.

Here in this first chapter of human history in Genesis, "the book of beginnings," we may note several beginnings: the first children, the first family life, the first vocations, the first worship mentioned, the first approach to God, not only outwardly, but more importantly, in the "hidden person of the heart." (1 Peter 3:4) Here we find also the first recorded communication with God since the blight of sin upon the human personality.

Undoubtedly, Adam had taught his sons about the altar and its necessary sacrifices for the forgiveness of sin. To stand before a Holy God, a person must recognize the redemptive value of that altar and the blood of the sin offering pointing to a future hour which tells the awesome depth of God's hatred for sin and also the wide and far reach of His love for the sinner.

When God met with the two young men standing before Him, He looked at their hearts, "that inner essential part of us that lies beyond the realm of matter," (Fredk A. Filby. "The Lord weighs the heart.")

"How does a right belief begin? A man must come to the Master, listen to His word, and do what He says. Then he will come to know God, and know that he knows Him." (from George MacDonald," Discovering the Character of God")

Just imagine how Adam's sons must have questioned their parents about God! And who could have better answered them in the thrilling measure that Adam and Eve had been instructed? For in the life of Adam and Eve, there continued to be an intimate knowledge of the Eternal Father. Their memory of what He had shown them must have been greater than any volumes treasured in libraries we consult today . . . Now, at this important turning point, would Adam's sons choose to love God as He so evidently loved them?

"The crown and joy of life is to desire and do the will of the eternal Source of will and of all life." ("Discovering the Character of God" p 51)

This day it appeared that both Cain and Abel acknowledged God in bringing their offerings, and in seeking to worship Him.

"Cain brought an offering of the fruit of the ground to the Lord, and Abel also brought of the firstlings of his flock and their fat. And the Lord respected Abel and his offering, but he did not respect Cain and his offering." (Genesis 4 : 3,4)

It is in the New Testament that we find out why Abel's offering was respected. The key word there is *faith.*

"Faith is the substance of things hoped for." (Heb. 12:1)

Faith takes hold of God's promise of hope. That hope is of redemption wrought for us in God's way, "foreordained before the foundation of the world". (1 Peter 1:20)

God's solution beginning to be worked out in Abel's day, stands presently true in every generation of mankind. Like God, His truth is eternal. Before history could tell the story of the Savior of the world, salvation was already effective via faith in the sacrifice for sin. Whoever chose to worship in reverence and humility, as God directed, could be found well pleasing unto Him.

Abel's faith drew into his heart not only God's forgiveness, but God Himself.

"By faith, Abel offered unto God a more excellent sacrifice than Cain, through which he obtained witness that he was righteous, God testifying of his gifts . . ." (Hebrews 11:4)

In contrast, Cain, with his offering not respected, became "very angry and his countenance fell." Instantly, God confronted Cain with a warning, for He sought to head him away from peril.

"Why are you angry? Why has your countenance fallen? If you do well, will you not be accepted? And if you do not well, sin lies at the door. And its desire is for you, but you should rule over it." (Genesis:4:7)

At this point, the first temptation recorded outside Eden is in progress. God who also loved Cain, sought to save him from the disaster just ahead. For God is "not willing that any should perish." (2 Peter 3:9)

Nevertheless He will not, even here, violate the freedom of the human will. As James writes in his New Testament epistle,

"Each one is tempted when he is drawn away by his own desires and enticed. Then when desire has conceived it gives birth to sin, and sin, when it is fully grown, brings forth death." (James 1:14,15)

Swiftly, the first crime in history is committed, and Cain murdered his brother Abel. Abel became the first martyr, for it was because of his faith that his jealous brother slew him.

Again the book of Hebrews brings into focus that altar where Abel touched God, and became a citizen of "the city of the living God." The passage in Hebrews

12:22-24 suddenly draws aside the curtain to reveal, in a flash, the presence of glory above,

"An innumerable company of angels, and the spirits of just men made perfect."

They are centered around the Mediator whose "blood of sprinkling" spoke "better things than that of Abel."

God's Lamb is "better than" Abel's sin offering. It is indeed better, as much better as the Reality is better than that which symbolizes it.

Abel became the first of God's new creation. Conformed now unto His image forever, the inner person, his immortal soul, had entered instantly into the indestructible Great House of the living God.

Words of wisdom from the book of Proverbs, written centuries after Abel, echo the truth he experienced:" In the way of righteousness is life.

"In its pathway there is no death."
(Proverbs 12:2 8)

To us, the faith of Abel is speaking yet in the words of the hymn:

"Mine is the sin, but thine the righteousness;
Mine the guilt, but Thine the cleansing blood;
Here is my robe, my refuge, and my peace:
Thy blood, Thy righteousness, O Lord My God."

(From "At the Lord's Table" by Horatius Bonar)

# Can It Be?

Can it be Thou hast designed
My soul to mirror Thee?
Though in a mortal frame confined,
Thy Life my liberty,
To walk with Thee arrayed in light
Enjoy Thy garden of delight
All day and all night long.

Teach me the language of Thine heart
My spirit in Thy likeness made,
Would see Thee, Savior, as Thou art,
My thoughts upon Thee stayed.
Thy Presence is my dwelling-place;
My joy to look upon Thy face,
My gladness, and my song.

# Chapter Four

## The Rapture of a Saint

"Watch therefore for you do not know what
hour your Lord is coming." (Matthew 24:42)

Early Genesis, chapter five, begins like a
document of genealogies. But a careful look
at it discloses, against a report of births, of
progeny and deaths, a unique account of one man, the
seventh generation from Adam, who stands tall and
upright. He is the epitome of God's original intention
for man whom He created.

The chapter begins with the statement: "In the day
that God created man, He made him in the likeness of
God." Here is God's intent, "the meaning of a man," as
George MacDonald expresses it. Like a *perfect* rose is
the meaning of a rose—that which the Creator means it
to be, so this one man typifies God's plan.

From Adam comes the succession following the line
of Seth, Enosh, Cainan, Mahalaleel, Jared—the closing
phrase about each is, "and he died." Then, in the same
format, comes Enoch, son of Jared. He lived sixty-five
years and begat Methuselah. But at this point, the
predictable order changes: "After he begot Methusaleh,
*Enoch walked with God* three hundred years and begat
sons and daughters."

"Enoch walked with God."

We are reminded of that Garden walk with God, where Adam and Eve knew fellowship with God at the beginning of human history.

In the beginning was God. God says of Himself, "I am Alpha", the beginning. He is the Alpha of Time. He is also the Omega, the ending of Time.

Enoch walked with God as Adam had, but with a significant difference. Adam and Eve's environment was in the innocency and purity of the Garden of the Lord. But Enoch's society was, in majority, ungodly, when mankind was drifting rapidly into "the way of Cain" who "went out from the presence of the Lord to dwell in the land of wanderings", purposelessness.

At sixty-five years of age, Enoch chose to walk with God. The milestone of that crisis is the birth of Methuselah, his first-born son. What happened to turn Enoch's eyes upon his Maker? How is it that he decided to "lift up his heart to the Heart from whence he came?" ("Cries of the Heart," by Ravi Zechariah)

Was it that Enoch was given the prophetic insight of impending judgment, and that by the end of his son's lifetime, it would fall upon the world? Some students of Scripture, like E.H. Pember who wrote EARTH'S EARLIEST AGES, say that the name, Methuselah, signifies that "when he dies, it shall come."

We know also, that in the years Enoch walked on earth with God, he preached earnestly to warn his generation of God's coming judgment upon the ungodly. His words were graphic: ". . . to execute judgment on all, to convict all who are ungodly . . . of all their ungodly deeds which they have committed in an ungodly way, and of all the harsh things which ungodly sinners have spoken against Him." (Jude 15)

It is interesting that Methusaleh's years were more than those of any other person. He lived 969 years, "and he died." God waited long and patiently, yearning for people to turn back to Him . . . Methuselah's life span would bring him to the brink of the Great Flood.

"Behold the Lord comes with ten thousands of His saints," Enoch proclaimed. (Jude 14)


In these words, he sees far beyond the time of Noah, his great grandson, to the triumphant conclusion of history. He saw the God who is Omega, the Ending, opening the back door of Time upon a new creation "wherein dwells righteousness." And where morning never changes into evening, for "there is no night there." (Rev. 21:25)

Here again is the light of Hope beaconing down the ages of history to promise final conquest over evil. God gave this Hope to Adam and Eve in Eden, and now again to Enoch who lived in a day when Adam had so recently died.

"The secret of the Lord is with those that fear Him." (Psalm 25:14)

We may also contemplate the truth that God knows the End from the Beginning. History flows onward, not by chance nor accident, but structured by the eternal purposes of God.

> Eternity with all its years,
> Stands present in Thy view;
> To Thee there's nothing old appears,
> Great God there's nothing new. (An old hymn)

"Enoch walked with God three hundred years." Thinking of the powerful undertow of Enoch's generation, we marvel at his consistent witness, living in communion with God, acknowledging Him in all things: mundane duties, family relationships, all the cross-current difficulties and trials of the human condition. Like Brother Lawrence, "he practiced the presence of God."

"The more we truly know God, the more we will desire Him, until at length we live in and for Him with all our conscious heart." (George MacDonald, "Discovering the Character of God" by Michael Phillios, Bethany House)

Enoch reached out to people, and urged them to turn from ungodliness. He knew that God would not deal with evil by merely punishing it, but He must destroy it. Toward the sinner His judgment could be redemptive to all who would repent. But God would not continue to allow corruption to prevail. He must cleanse it away.

What Enoch experienced in walking day by day with God is relevant to us today. God was his significant circumstance in a world of desperate corruption, violence, perversion, blasphemous rejection of God. The times were perilous. The Future, growing darker. Yet Enoch, walking near to God, felt the Divine Companion's grief over mankind throbbing in his soul. In loving God, he exercised that same love in concern for others, the people of his own generation, pleading with them to turn to God. Walking with God did not hide him away from the crisis of his day. Walking with God, to Enoch, meant all out dedication to His will.

Malcolm Muggeridge gives us much to think about in his statement of the purpose of God for us:

"The true purpose of our existence in this world is, quite simply, to look for God, and in looking, to find Him, and in having found Him, to love Him, thereby establishing a harmonious relationship with His purposes for His creation." (Twentieth Century Testimony by Thomas Howard)

Thinking of Enoch, we must realize that he had
no written Scriptures, only the documentary records
of Adam and seven generations after him, and then
only that of the line of Seth. He had word-of-mouth
information, of course, especially of man's unique
place among all other creatures, as that of God's
image in him. This was shown by his conscience that
registered guilt for wrong-doing, and directed the
guileless to goodness instead of evil, to light rather
than darkness, to worship instead of independence
of God.

Enoch also had the intense awareness of God's
presence with him. The more he walked with God the
more he learned of Him, and knowing Him, he knew
the delight and joy of living to please Him, of doing
His will.

Enoch found the sacred gladness of enjoying God,
and he also discovered the precious truth that God
delighted to commune with Him.

"The prayer of the upright is His delight." (Proverbs
15:8b)

Many others could have been like Enoch. God's
great welcome is to everyone who wills to come to Him.
God is never partial. His invitation is to all.

Next we come to the most astounding historical
statement about Enoch. Instead of stating that he lived
so many years and died, the text reads:

"And Enoch walked with God, and he was not, for
God took him.

Read it again. Think about it. Enoch did not die!
He wonderfully circumvented death. He by-passed
"the way of all flesh." Enoch did not die, he was
raptured!

"By faith Enoch was translated so that he did not
see death, and was not found, because God had

translated him, for before his translation he had this testimony, that he pleased God." (Hebrews 11:5)

In "The Celestial Country", Bernard of Cluny says,
"Thou wilt not leave us in the dust,
Thou madest man he knows not why;
He thinks he was not meant to die,
And Thou hast made him, Thou art just."

One day, after that fifteen-score years on earth, Enoch, aged and stooped, halting and dimly seeing, leaning heavily on his Divine Companion, heard Him say,

"We've come to sunset here, and a step away is sunrise at my House. Come home with me."

And as Enoch entered the gates of his heavenly home, a great change took place. He left off his dusty garment, and suddenly was provided a beautiful enduring one, appropriate for his new dwelling. He was now equipped to see and behold at last the One he knew so well.

Bernard of Cluny speaks of this experience in his joyous poem, The Celestial Country.

But He whom now we trust in
Shall then be seen and known;
And they that know and see Him
Shall have Him as their own.

In all the millenniums in the history of mankind, only two people thus far have been raptured: Enoch and Elijah. Although physical death for the believer is but the avenue unto God-visible and His everlasting kingdom, Enoch, who was taken out of a world on the brink of the great Deluge, stands before us as a preview

or type, of another rapture foretold often in the New
Testament.

Many times we have heard Scriptures read at
funerals; sometimes they sound unreal. And yet, the
very Hope that Enoch saw happening at the far edge of
Time, we are also given to know as the "Blessed Hope
of His appearing." (Titus 2:13)

"Behold, I tell you a mystery (secret); we shall not
all sleep (die) but we shall be changed, in a moment, in
the twinkling of an eye." (1Cor. 15: 51,52)

"We shall be caught up to meet the Lord in the air, and
thus we shall always be with the Lord." (1 Thess. 4:17)

Enoch speaks to this event both in his preaching and
in his life. The joy of God's purpose for all who walk
by faith, is ours in the love, force, and certitude of His
own words to us.

"I go to prepare a place for you. And if I go and
prepare a place for you, I will come again and receive
you to myself, that where I am, there you may be also."
(John 14:3)

So it is, that via death or translation, when "absent from
the body" we are "present with the Lord." (2 Cor. 5:8)

Unlike the Adam of Eden, it was by faith that Enoch
walked with God. Faith brought into his life forgiveness
of sin, and even victory over it, while God taught him
to walk "in paths of righteousness for his name's sake."
(Psalm 23:3)

For us, as for every generation in history, God is the
God of Hope. The example of Enoch walking with God
was not to be unique, but the norm for us today. We are
created, and then re-created by faith, to walk with God.
We journey, not toward evening, but toward morning
so that in His likeness we will stand before Him with
His own righteousness, His own merit. We are
"accepted in the Beloved" (Eph. 1:6).

By faith, Enoch pleased God. "Without faith it is impossible to please Him. For He that comes to God must believe that He is, and that He is a rewarder of those that diligently seek Him." (Hebrews 11:6)

Enoch's rapture declares the reality of immortality, because He lives in the presence of the God of the living, the Father of spirits, and Source of everlasting life.

Enoch knew the best of Eden, even on earth, and so may we, in the exalted privilege that is ours, to walk with God by faith. We too do rejoice in the Hope of "His appearing."

# Do We Not Hear Thy Footfall?

Do we not hear Thy footfall, O Beloved,
Among the stars on many a moonless night?
Do we not catch the whisper of thy coming
On winds of dawn, and often in the light
Of noontide and of sunset almost see Thee?
Look up through shining air
And long to see Thee, O Beloved, long to see Thee
And wonder that Thou art not standing there?

And we shall hear Thy footfall, O Beloved,
And starry ways will open, and the night
Will call her candles from their distant stations,
And winds shall sing Thee, noon, and mingled light
Of rose-red evening thrill with lovely welcome,
And we, caught up in air,
Shall see Thee, O Beloved, we shall see Thee,
In hush of adoration see Thee there.

Amy Wilson Carmichael.

(From "A Sacrifice of Praise" edited by James H.
Trott, Cumberland House Publishers, Nashville, Tennessee)

# Chapter Five

## Noah Walked With God

"And those who know Your Name will
put their trust in You." Psalm 9:10

Only two millenniums of human history had passed when the Genesis account reveals the tragedy of unchecked iniquity on the earth. "Then the Lord saw that the wickedness of man was great in the earth, and that every intent of the thoughts of his heart was only evil continually." (Gen. 6:5)

God's beloved handiwork had self-destructed.

"For in the image of God He made Man."

Then follows the statement of the anguish in God's heart.

"And the Lord was sorry," the word here is *Asah*, grieved, pierced, "as in taking a deep breath in extreme pain". With heart-piercing sorrow, God looked upon the earth. It is as though God wept.

"My Spirit shall not strive with man forever." (Gen. 6:3)

Weeping. Yet waiting still. For many decades Enoch's long and powerful witness had pleaded with his generation. Methusaleh yet lived and would not pass off the scene until the very precipice of judgement. He was a constant reminder of impending punishment.

By faith, the son of Methusaleh, Lamech, named his firstborn *Noah*, meaning "Rest", saying:

"This one will comfort us concerning our work and toil of our hands, because of the ground which the Lord has cursed." (Gen. 5:29).

Lamech's faith reached out beyond the Great Deluge unto a day at a new altar and a renewed earth when "the God of hope" would pledge,

"I will never again curse the ground for man's sake." (Gen. 6:12)

But now, "God looked upon the earth and saw that all flesh had corrupted its way upon the earth." And God said,

"The end of all flesh has come before Me." (Gen. 6:12,13) God spoke these words to the one individual who was the exception to this stark summary of mankind.

"However Noah found grace in the eyes of the Lord." (Gen. 6:8)

Here is the startling contrast, an upright man like God had created man to be, profiled in white, as it were, against the darkness of undiluted evil in his own generation.

"Noah was a just man, perfect in his generation. *Noah walked with God*" (Gen. 6:9)

Noah knew God in present day by day communication, in everyday speech, and with explicit instructions to be heeded and acted upon. Noah led his family in his example of faith. The secret of his inner life was his listening to God. He kept thinking God-ward, and looking God-ward amid the confusing swirl of godless attitudes, and of rebellion against the Lord.

"In God's heart, in His very Being, lies our hope, our deliverance." (George MacDonald, "Discovering the Character of God" page 194 by Michael Phillips, Bethany House Publishers.)

This became Noah's assurance as he understood God's grace in providing for his escape from judgment for both himself and all his family.

"And God said to Noah, 'The earth is filled with violence, And behold I shall destroy them with the earth . . . Make yourself an Ark of gopher wood . . . And this is how you shall make it . . . And behold, I Myself am bringing a flood of waters upon the earth to destroy from under heaven all flesh in which, is the breath of life.'" (Gen. 6:13-15)

"But I will establish My Covenant with you; and you shall go into the Ark" (Gen.6:18)

Noah's encounter with God, his Maker, was tangible, audible, the living, breathing, primary truth of his consciousness. Though God spoke of future, unseen events, Noah was convinced of their certainty. Therefore, his faith obeyed. The faith of Noah is defined in the New Testament as "godly fear".

"By faith Noah, being divinely warned of things not yet seen, moved with godly fear, prepared an Ark to the saving of his household, by which he condemned the world, and became heir of the righteousness which is according to faith." (Heb. 11:7)

In the common, seeable, predictable life around him, Noah must *walk with God by faith*. As time went on, his peers, no doubt, scoffed and jeered at him. Yet he followed God's detailed instructions. The task was formidable. It would take him 120 years to finish it. Noah was the oddity of the Century, a man obsessed with building a huge ship, three stories high, on dry land upon ground that had never seen rain or storm, for it was watered by the morning mists adequate for all its vegetation and life.

Noah's deep sense of the present God held him steadfast, following God's directions one at a time.

"This Noah did according to all that the Lord commanded him. So did he." (Gen. 6:22)

His work, day by day, into the years and decades became the evangel, to the world of his generation, urging repentance before certain judgment fell. All the long, long time the Ark was being built, the Spirit of God kept pleading, the long-suffering of God kept waiting, the heart of God, who is Savior, kept on calling, "Come unto Me and rest." (Matt. 11:28)

More than a hundred years Noah labored, and by his work he preached righteousness. But there came a limit to God's waiting . . . "Keep the day of judgement in mind all the while," reads the Epistle of Barnabas. (120 ad). "It will sharpen your determination to work for God, either by the words you speak, or by the effort of your hands." (from "Faith Under Fire", Day 69, by David Winters, Shaw Publishers, Wheaton, Illinois)

Then came the morning when Noah heard God's voice commanding,

"Come into the Ark, you and your household, for I have seen that you are righteous before Me in this generation." (Gen. 7:1)

Clear directions were given and carried out Again, God spoke,

"For after seven days, I will cause it to rain on the earth forty days and forty nights, and I will destroy from off the face of the earth all living things that I have made." (Genesis 7:4)

God had not told Noah to *go* into the Ark, but He had said, "*Come* into the Ark" For God Himself was inside. The "God of hope" was in the Ark with Noah and all his family along with the living creatures that were to be preserved. The only window in the ship looked upward. "And God shut them in." (Gen. 7:16)

As the great roar of God's wrath began, not just torrents from the sky, but also the fountains of the deep were broken up. And subterranean waters were unleashed in volume and indescribable upheaval. The complete corruption of man had been worse than anyone can imagine. The destruction was necessary.

Lifted higher and higher upon the agitated waters, the Ark rode safely through the Deluge which covered the earth's highest peaks. That solitary ship, safe upon a vast destruction, pictured God's outlasting mercy as well as His holy intolerance of sin.

Inside the Ark, the family of Noah must wait a whole year for the waters to recede until the dry land once more appeared. All the while, this small remnant of humanity were at rest upon the great Deep of God's unchanging grace.

"Be still and know that I am God." (Psalm 46:10)

To Noah, the voice of the Eternal was known and familiar. What thoughts must have been his in these days? Beneath the outward in-ship routines of caring for each other and the animals as well, he must have had great thoughts of God, His nearness, his salvation.

"We cannot lose ourselves where all is home.,
Nor drift away from Thee
Thy greatness makes us brave as children are
When those they love are near." (F W Faber,The Greatness of God)

"You are my Hiding-place.
You will protect me from trouble,
And surround me with songs of deliverance." (Psalm 32:7)

"And the waters prevailed on earth one hundred and fifty days". (Gen.7:24)

The Ark rested upon one of the peaks of the high ranges in Armenia, on Ararat at 16,916 feet. At last, God directed Noah, his wife, his sons, and their wives, with all the animals preserved in pairs and sevens, out of the Ark as He had so carefully guided them into it and shut the door.

Now, outdoors again, what gladness, what joy it must have been for them to emerge upon a shining new earth, cleansed and sparkling in color and beauty once more. In His soul Noah rested deeply in the God of hope-fulfilled, and also of hope beckoning unto tomorrow.

"For I know the plans I have for you, declares the Lord, plans to prosper you and not to harm you, plans to give you hope and a future. Then will you call upon me and come and pray to me, and I will listen to you. You will seek me, and find me when you seek for me with all your heart." (Jer. 29:11-13)

The first act of Noah as he began life anew upon a land washed of all defilement, was to build an altar to the Lord, a truly propitiatory sacrifice, and to lift up his hands in prayer.

"The highest expression of faith is not prayer in its ordinary sense of petition, but prayer in its sublimest expression of praise." (Wesley L. Ducarel)

"Then will I go to the altar of God, unto God, my exceeding joy" or "the gladness of my joy." (Psalm 43:4)

With a joyful heart Noah patterned to his family the habit of worship.

"As God dwells in your thoughts, you will be worshiping, and God will be accepting. We know what God wants us to be. He wants us to be worshipers." (A.W. Tozer)

"Worship is the supreme expression in life, the root from which life's branches grow and expressions flower." (Ravi Zacharias "Cries of the Heart")

With Noah and his family at rest in the mercy of God, the new world was revived. It began with mankind once more in sync with the heart of the Creator, the Eternal saving, loving Lord God. And arching in the sky above the altar and its offering of peace with God, Noah saw the first rainbow fracturing gloriously all the colors of light, its eight-fold spectrum, painting in the sky the components of light itself.

And he heard again the voice he knew so well, pledging His covenant. The rainbow signed the Covenant with all mankind:

"It shall be, when I bring a cloud over the earth, that the rainbow shall be seen in the cloud, and I will remember my covenant which is between me and you and every living creature of all flesh; the waters shall never again become a flood to destroy all flesh." (Gen. 9:11)

Once more history begins with man in harmony with God, and enlightened in fellowship and communion with Him. In such a context the Scriptures again emphasize the value of human life.

"For in the image of God He made man." (Gen. 9:6)

And because Noah had chosen to walk with God, the history of mankind continued. Even though in stating His covenant with Noah, God said,

"The imagination of man's heart is evil from his youth",

Yet in spite of the fact that mankind tended to drift away from the true and living God, He would not ever cease in His pursuit of them. For God so loved, and so desired everyone to be rescued from Evil.

Each individual choosing Him was most precious to God's heart. For had He not created them to desire Him? Through the centuries, God's purpose and work of redemption would not cease, nor would it exclude any person who even began to seek his mercy. God is impartial. His compassion for them that seek Him is as unwavering and unchanging as God Himself is, the Eternal Father, Son, and Spirit, the Triune Deity.

Others follow Abel, Enoch, and Noah, on into every life span and time, "that multitude no man can number." (Revelation 7:9)

The eldest son of Noah whose name was Shem had a son called Uz. He and his progeny lived in a territory named for him. The next Portrait of this era of "the Beginnings" is that of "a man in the Land of Uz whose name was Job." He was known as the "greatest of all the people of the East," and it was the Lord Himself who spoke of this one as "My Servant Job."

Job's book, an epic drama written in poetry except for its introduction and conclusion, is the oldest writing of all the scriptures, probably penned by Job himself. It is the first of the books of Poetry in the Bible, and placed in the category of Wisdom Literature.

Though its title is *Job*, the central Person of the book is the God of Job Whom we have found in Genesis, and will find again in awesome dimensions in the story of "My Servant Job".

At the time of Abram, living in Ur of the Chaldees, this, another who served God lived in the land of Uz, in country northeast of Mesopotamia where God first appeared to Abram. So it is that Job, like Abraham, belongs to the Patriarchal era, the period of the Genesis, the Beginnings.

Job show s us the God of the stars, and brings into focus the Great Creator Who is our living Redeemer in Time and Eternity.

# Call Him Father

Would'st dare to call Him Father

Who hung the worlds in space?

Of Whom the Light eternal

Is His Dwelling place?


Cans't dare to call Him Father

That holiest One above

Ah yes, we call Him Father

Because His Name is Love.

# Gladness of My Joy

Gladness of my joy Thou art today
Song of life, in every hour, my stay,
Focus of my gaze upon Thy Face,
Substance of my hope, Thy saving Grace,
Seated in the heavenlies with Thee,
Living in Thy presence, victory.
Blessing from the Father as I pray,
Gladness of my joy Thou art today.

# Mere Edges of His Ways

He stretches the north over empty space;
He hangs the earth on nothing.
He binds up the waters in His thick clouds,
Yet the clouds are not broken under it.
He covers the face of His throne,
And spreads His cloud over it.
He drew a circular horizon on the face of the waters,
At the boundary of light and darkness.
The pillars of heaven tremble,
And are astonished at His reproof.
He stirs up the sea with His power,
And by His understanding He breaks up the storm.
By His Spirit He adorned the heavens;
His hand pierced the fleeing serpent.
Indeed these are the mere edges of His ways,
And how small a whisper do we hear of Him!
But the thunder of His power who can understand?

Job 26: 7-14

## "Where Can Wisdom Be Found?"

But where can wisdom be found?
And where is the place of understanding?
Man does not know its value,
Nor is it found in the land of the living.
The deep says, "It is not in me,"
And the sea says, "It is not with me."
It cannot be purchased for gold,
Nor can silver be weighed for its price.

From whence then does wisdom come?
And where is the place of understanding?
It is hidden from the eyes of all living,
And concealed from the birds of the air.
Death and Destruction say,
"We have heard a report about it with our ears."
God understands its way,
And He knows its place.
For He looks to the ends of the earth,
And sees under the whole heavens.

. . . .

Then He saw wisdom and declared it;
He prepared it, indeed, He searched it out.
And to man He said,
"Behold, the fear of the Lord, that is wisdom,
And to depart from evil is understanding."

Job 28:12-15; 20-24; 27,28

# Chapter Six

## My Servant Job

"Behold, the fear of God, that is wisdom,
and to depart from evil is understanding."
Job 28:28

"There was a man in the land of Uz whose name was Job" so begins the oldest book in the Bible, and one of profound value in content. This first of the books known as Wisdom Literature, centers upon God Himself. Job leads us from beholding the "edges of His ways" to revealing His character and awesome attributes. At last Job shows us that God is indispensable in our lives.

"The very Life of God by which we live is an everlasting eternal giving of Himself away." (George MacDonald "Discovering The Character Of God" by Michael Phillips)

When His Servant Job is denuded of all else, He clings tenaciously to God Who is his very meaning and Breath of life. Job brings us closer and closer until at last he leads us face to face with Him. In His awesome but tender presence, Job is fully satisfied, and humbled as he realizes the great Creator is also His beloved Deliverer, and His adored Master.

God does not rebuke Job, but rather, commends him in contrast to his wise friends who would bend the facts concerning Job to suit their own philosophy on the subject of human suffering.

Job's story that deals with matters too wonderful for prose presentation, is given to us in the exalted style of poetry, and narrated in drama, full of fervor and eloquence. It would take volumes to address the poignant content of this book which is introduced and concludes in prose to frame its setting for us.

But we can observe the person introduced by God as "My Servant, Job." And in doing so, we find Job leading us to God.


"Have you considered my servant Job that there is none like him in the earth, a blameless and upright man, one who fears God and shuns evil?"

The voice of the Lord is gladness as He speaks before His angels in the high court of heaven.

"The Lord has established His throne in Heaven.
And His kingdom rules over all (Psalm 103:19)."

"Bless the Lord among you His angels
Who excel in strength
Who do His Word
Heeding the voice of His Word.
Bless the Lord all you His Hosts
You minister of His who do His pleasure."
(Psalm 103:20, 21)

In the company of angels, the Lord spoke directly to the Dark Angel, Satan, who also stood before the Lord.

"Have you considered my servant Job?"

Thus is Job introduced in Heaven, "a blameless and upright man who fears God and shuns evil".

On earth as his book begins, Job is known among his peers as "a man who is blameless and upright, who fears God and shuns evil".

Seen of angels from above and esteemed on earth among his people, Job's record of integrity is described in identical words.

That Job was an historical figure is verified in the book of Ezekiel where he is mentioned along with Noah and Daniel. (Ezekiel 14:15,20).

Also James, in the New Testament comments,

"You have heard of the patience of Job" (James 5:11). The fact that he lived in the Land Of Uz indicates that he, like Abraham, is a descendant of Shem. Uz was the name of the grandson of Shem through his son, Aram. Abraham descended from Shem's son Arphaxad. Job, a contemporary of Abraham, lived in the patriarchal era in history. In the Land of Uz, Job was widely known.

"This man was the greatest of all the people of the East" (Job 1:3).

As his story begins, our first look at Job is photographic. He stands before the altar of sacrifice, robed in the status dress of an elder counselor in Uz. With his arms upraised and face aglow in the rising sun, Job worships his Maker and Redeemer, the Almighty God. As priest to his large family, Job begins each day with God. He intercedes for his seven sons and three daughters and their households "lest they sin and refuse to bless God in their hearts." With the smoke of the sin-offering rising with each dawn, the Lord watched, considered, and delighted in the man He called "My servant Job." This sheds a celestial light upon the concept of servant. It is the job description of angelic beings and of the heavenly hosts.

"His servants shall serve Him, and they shall see His face" (Rev. 22:4)

The title, servant conveys a royal vocation, a most holy calling, This is underscored in a startling way in the words of Malachi, the last book of the Old Testament. He writes:

"Then you shall again discern
Between the righteous and the wicked
Between one who serves God
And one who serves Him not." (Malachi 3:18)

The mystery behind this epic drama is revealed behind the scenes, with that question the Lord brought before Satan, the Antagonist of God and man. Satan's reply was his weapon of deadly doubt.

"Does Job fear God for nothing? . . . Touch his bone and flesh, and he shall surely curse You to Your face" (Job1:8,2:5)

The Adversary, ever seeking to hurt God by destroying His most beloved creation, wanted to prove that Job served God, not for God Himself, but for His benefits and blessings.

We are given understanding of the enigma of Job's story in the introduction when we are made aware of that ageless conflict between Good and Evil, between God and His Opposite, the Devil.

Yet God who is Omniscient knew Job's heart, and knew His servant Job would persevere in faith. God knew the outcome of the battle would, not only defeat the Enemy finally, but would lift Job to spiritual maturity finer than the purest gold. Job would then be able to reflect his Creator's likeness as never before.

No other book in Scripture deals with the problem of causeless suffering as does this unique first volume of Wisdom Literature. The substance of the book is alight with truths that have endured through the millenniums of Time, and are both pragmatic as well as profound It contains a breadth of knowledge even from the mind of the man named Job, that seems marvelous from his early place in time, only about ten generations from the day of Noah and the great Flood. The book contains one chapter given wholly to the pursuit of wisdom which ends with these lines:

"From where then does wisdom come? And where is the place of understanding?

And to man, He said, Behold, the fear of the Lord, that is wisdom,

And to depart from evil is understanding" (Job 28:20,28).

Job's life before disaster fell, before his unusual losses and suffering had begun, was like a pastoral music, softly expressing rest and contentment, a glad spirit, happy in God and His unfailing loving kindness. Job recognizes that

"The heart of the Eternal is most wonderfully kind" (Hymn—"There's A Wideness in God's Mercy" FW Faber)

He meditates upon God watching over him, His lamp upon his head, His light showing him the path at night, His counsel in his dwelling. Job sensed and believed in El Shaddai, the God Who is sufficient, the Almighty. Like Abraham, this name for God is the one Job used most often.

Job thanks God for wisdom to help and counsel his fellow man; for allowing him to benefit the poor, to be eyes to the blind, to be feet to the lame, consolation to the widows, and to rescue victims of crime. God has privileged him to serve others and to make a great difference in the land of Uz This was the beautiful music of "the law of kindness", the sacred trust from God to "love thy neighbor as thyself."

Without cause, the pastoral strains are interrupted. A sudden discordant transition crashes upon Job. He is unaware of *why*.

A day that began with Job walking as usual in the
smile of God, turned suddenly black with the
unthinkable. Swiftly, one upon the heels of the other,
runners came to the widespread tents of Job with evil
tidings. The first cried in alarm,

"The Sabeans raided your oxen and donkeys with
all the servants, I alone escaped!"

Another came while the first was still speaking, with
the shout,

"Fire from Heaven burned up the sheep and their
shepherds." The third cried,

"The Chaldeans took away your camels and killed
your servants, all save myself."

A fourth runner told of a desert whirlwind that swept
away all of Job's sons and daughters and their
households. In one day, Job had lost everything!

"Job arose and tore his robe and shaved his head,
and fell to the ground and worshiped." (Job 1:20)

His first words were to the One most cherished
whose Breath he breathed, whose Being was inexorably
annealed to his own soul.

> "Naked I came from my mother's womb
> And naked shall I return there.
> The Lord gave and the Lord has taken away.
> Blessed be the Name of the Lord" (Job1:21).

"In all this, Job did not sin with his lips, or charge
God with wrong." (Job 1:22)

As traumatic as this day had been, there would come
yet another soon after.

"Then Satan went out from the presence of the Lord
and struck Job with boils from the sole of his feet to the
crown of his head" (Job 2:7)

Upon this final stroke of misfortune, Job "took for

himself a potsherd with which to scrape himself while he sat in the midst of ashes" (Job 2:8).

At this point his intimate and closest friend, his own wife, failed him.

"Do you still hold to your integrity? Curse God and die!" (Job 2:8)

But he said to her, "You speak as one of the foolish women speaks, shall we accept good from God, and should we not accept adversity" (Job 2:10)? "In all this did not Job sin with his lips (Job 2:11)."

At this point it seems Job has been stripped of everything, yet there is more loss for him yet to come.

Job's three wise friends had come from their own lands to visit Job in his extreme misery and to comfort him. As they sit on the ground beside him in silence for seven days, the narrative introduction closes, and gives way to poetry, suspenseful, probing into the problem of pain and adversity, the mystery of suffering in human experience.

The epic drama is alive with fire and zeal and poetic power. It's beauty and eloquence is unmatched in any literature of any era or language. Written originally in Hebrew, its poetry, exalted and majestic, is in Hebrew parallelism, and is of the highest literary and intellectual merit. It deals with enigma in searching out the why of suffering and tragedy, and many unanswered questions can only be resolved in the vision of God Himself, the grand climax of the drama. He is found to be immanent in all His creation, and deeply caring, although He is also transcendent, the Author of Time and all things. He was there already when

"the morning stars sang together, and the sons of God shouted for joy." (Job 38:7)

As we focus on Job in his persevering faith, we cannot tarry in the many awesome passages describing creation and the works of God. The exciting search for wisdom in chapter twenty-eight, the rich illuminating statements of truth both outward and inward throughout the book, but we will need also to walk with Job in the depths of his misery and darkness.

He is further deprived by the alienation of his magi friends. They are convinced that suffering is caused by commensurate sin. Nor can they imagine any reason for such disasters as those Job has been experiencing unless Job has been guilty of some secret wickedness. Some serious crime must be the provocation of his awesome calamity! To pursue their theory, they keep battering Job with words of suspicion and even slander that strip him of all self esteem, and destroy his reputation among his own people.

Finally, Job, as though naked, is left forsaken and alone with nothing except himself and God. His grip on God is unbreakable. Job will not disown God despite the terrifying contradiction that seemingly revokes His Name, El Shaddai. Job refuses to let go of God. Despite his own "multitude of words" without answers, and the awesome unknown "too wonderful" for him, Job cries

> "Why do I take my flesh in my teeth,
> And put my life in my hands?
> Though He slay me, yet will I trust Him!
> Even so I will defend my own ways before Him.
> He also shall be my salvation (Job 13:14-16)."

There is significant rhythm in this drama. Job walks us with him into the deep vales of contemplation, even despair. Then he suddenly leaps up to the glorious truth of God as though Someone has lighted the candle of his own spirit, and the flame reaches upward to touch the Face of God.

"Have pity upon me, have pity upon me,
O you, my friends,
For the hand of God has struck me!
Why do you persecute me as God does,
And are not satisfied with my flesh?
Oh, that my words were written!
Oh, that they were inscribed in a book!
That they were engraved on a rock
With an iron pen and lead forever!
For *I know that my Redeemer lives*,
And He shall stand up at last upon the earth;
And after my skin is destroyed, this I know,
That in my flesh I shall see God,
Whom I shall see for myself,
And my eyes shall behold, and not another.
How my heart yearns within me!" (Job 19:21-27)

Even throughout his volatile emotions, Job leads us steadily onward to the Heart of God, our Maker, The Almighty.

"Oh, that I knew where I might find Him!", he pleads, "That I might come even to His seat!" (Job 23:3)

"Look, I go forward, but He is not there,
And backward but I cannot perceive Him
When He works on the left hand, I cannot behold Him
When He turns to the right hand, I cannot see Him.
But he knows the way that I take;
When He has tested me,
I shall come forth as gold." (Job 23:8-10)

George MacDonald expresses Job's petition here when he observes that

"It is not what God can give us, but God Himself that we want." (p 179, "Discovering the Character of God" by Michael Phillips)

The epic poem is composed of three cycles of speeches, Job beginning them, and answering each in succession until the debate finally ceases.

"The words of Job are ended" (Job 31:40)

We have felt the pathos in Job's controversy with his three friends who have attempted to fit his circumstances into their contention that all suffering is punishment for sin. On the other hand, Job in honesty must defend his own integrity. How could he deny the record of God in his life? At the same time, his soul is unable to understand God in His out-of-character assault upon His own handiwork. In his questionings because of this, Job has come near to defending himself at God's disadvantage, and for this he is gently rebuked by both Elihu and the Voice of God. Job could not fathom mysteries "too wonderful" for him. He was not innocent of "hiding counsel by words without knowledge."

After the debate between Job and his three friends is finished, Elihu comes into center stage and begins to speak with conviction and wisdom although he is younger, and has respectfully waited until the four elders have ceased speaking. It was he who asked why not one of them had sought out Him

"Who gives songs in the night".(Job 35:10)

Elihu acts as a bridge between The great Debate and God. He severely rebukes the three friends of Job, saying,

"I paid close attention to you, and surely not one of you convinced Job, or answered his words (Job 32:12)."

Elihu portrays God's redemptive love in His habitual effort to rescue individuals from "going down into the Pit". In graphic poetry he emphasizes God's desire that "not any should perish", and Elihu also stresses the impartial character of God.

His speech, like a trumpet with no uncertain sound, heralds the triumphant finale of this symphonic Drama. Elihu begins a description of the gathering storm in which its whirlwind and thunder, and "His lightnings to the end of the earth" announce the very Presence of God. At last God Himself is there! The search is over.

"Hear attentively to the thunder of His Voice!" (Job 36:22).
"He thunders with His majestic voice." (Job 37:14)
"He comes from the North as golden splendour (Job 37:32)."

When suddenly God appears to Job in the whirlwind, the thunder has become the Voice of His word. "Then God answered Job out of the whirlwind and said:" (Job 38:1)

"Who is this who darkens counsel
By words without knowledge?
Now prepare yourself like a man;
I will question you, and you shall answer Me
(Job 38:3),"

It is interesting here that God alludes to a very confident statement Job had made earlier, when he declared:

"For He is not a man, as I am, that I may answer Him. (Job 9:32)."

We may even detect a Divine humor in this correction of Job's assertion. And then God begins the thrilling questions that direct His servant Job to give rapt attention to most marvelous revelations of Himself, Job's beloved Creator, His Master Whom to obey is his most sublime joy.

"Where were you when I laid
the foundations of the earth?
When the morning stars sang together
And all the sons of God shouted for joy?
Have you commanded the morning since
your days began,
And caused the dawn to know its place
(Job 38: 4.7,12)?"
Who has put wisdom in the mind?
Or Who has given understanding to the heart
(Job 38:36)?"

Though God does not address any of Job's
questions, His questions to Job are like arrows of light
that pierce open new vistas of enlightening so that Job
finds consummate Answers in God Himself. At last
beholding God, Job is swallowed up into the Divine
Answer to the searching of his soul. Job then humbly
talks to God.

"I have heard of You by he hearing of the ear,
But now my eye sees You.

Therefore I abhor myself
And repent in dust and ashes." (Job 42:5,6)

Before the Eternal, Job is humbled. "I repent in
dust". Before the Almighty, Job is lifted up. "I know
that You can do everything, and that no purpose of
Yours can be withheld from You." (Job 42:2)
The triumph of Job's faith in God, has vindicated
His servant Job, for God accepted him. And the Dark
Angel, Satan, has been forced to bow out in total defeat.
As for Job's three mistaken friends, they were twice
severely rebuked, for God said, "You have not spoken
of Me the thing that is right as My servant Job has."

Job's first act of obedience now was to go to the altar and intercede for Eliphaz, Bildad, and Zophar who had wronged him so acutely.

Afterward God restored his losses twofold, even giving him another seven sons and three daughters to belong to him on earth as did the former in heaven.

In the triumphant music of enduring faith, Job leads us to see God, his Answer and ours. Job has witnessed to us the truth St. Augustine discovered also,

"that he is happy who possesses God . . . Grace governs life by giving a supreme joy in the supremacy of God." (St. Augustine from ("The Legacy of Sovereign Joy", John Piper)

> *My servant Job has spoken of Me*
> *That which is right.*
> *Wounded sore, he trusts Me yet,*
> *By seeing without sight.*
> *My servant Job has found Me,*
> *The Dwelling-place of Light.*
> *Myself his Sovereign Answer*
> *The stars sing through the night.*

## Job's Faith

The multitude of words that darken light
Were mine, of grief and gloom, so dark the night
Then the candle of the Lord within my soul
Began to flame with Truth quick to control,
To brush away my doubts and make me know
My Witness is in heaven, and below
The fiery trials that are mine today
Are my Divine Creator's chosen way
Fraught with weights of glory yet untold.
He purposed these fires to melt and mold,
Bring forth my faith in purest gold.
I know that my Redeemer lives and waits
To welcome me into immortal gates
Of golden splendor and of Life indeed,
To see His face and know Him, from shackles freed
Even now God is my essential part
Maker, Beloved fulness of my heart.

# God of the Way

God of the Way that no fowl knoweth
Nor vulture's eye hath seen
God of the dark and secret places
Of fires that are clean,
God of Eternal "Weights of Glory"
That places of sapphires hold
God of The Way that walks through trial
And cometh forth in gold,
The song that hides my life in Thee
Is that Thou, Savior, seest me.

## Secret Place of Thunder

From the secret place of thunder
I heard the Voice of God.

His lightnings tore asunder
Dark palisades of Night
Revealing vistaed wonder
of uncreated Light.

From the secret place of thunder
I saw the Face of God.

The sackcloth weight of sadness
My Savior took away,
To clothe me with the gladness
of His unending Day.

In the secret place of thunder
I found the Arms of God.

# Chapter Seven

## The Friend of God

"Abraham rejoiced to see My day." Jesus Christ
(John 8:56)

In the prayer of King Jehosaphat of Judah at a time of extreme crisis, he brings before the Lord His Covenant promises to "Abraham, Thy friend forever" (2 Chronicles 20:8)

And this great fact is the portrait of Abraham told in twelve chapters of the book of Genesis. The gist of this story is that "Abraham believed God. And it was accounted unto him as righteousness. And he was called the friend of God." (James 2:23). It is a saga of a person to person walk with God, of faith proving itself by obedience, of devotion to the One Who had called him unto an everlasting friendship with Himself. The God of Glory had appeared to Abram in Mesopotamia, and ever since, God had become the beloved Sovereign of his life. The faith of Abraham was demonstrated in his immediate unhesitating obedience to the expressed will of God.

One of the most beautiful scenes in the biography of Abraham is of the aged friend of God, now ninety-nine years old, sitting in his tent door in the heat of the day, near the grove of terebinth trees at Mamre in Hebron.

Since the last visit of the Lord with him had been

only days ago, Abraham must have been thinking of
His recently spoken assurances:

"I am Almighty God, (El Shaddai) walk before Me,
and be blameless." (Genesis 17:1)

In other words, God was telling Abraham that He
Himself was his sufficiency. Abraham had then, with
dismay, reminded God that he was now getting old,
and yet did not have the promised heir. Then God had
answered him by declaring that He would make him
the father of many nations and peoples.

Today at his large array of tents, Abraham with an
insistent faith, a hope against hope, that struggled
against the tangible, solid here and now, felt himself
buoyed up by a strong premonition that something
wonderful was afoot.

He had no written scriptures, but in other ways God
had spoken to Him, revealing His heart and purposes.
That first personal encounter with His Creator, whom
he knew as the Most High God, Possessor of heaven
and earth, occurred in Ur of the Chaldeans, where he
and Sarai, his wife, lived at that time.

It was a great city, and prosperous. He himself was
rich in livestock and silver and gold. But Abram and
Sarai were childless, and also distinctly out of fashion
with the mores of their society. Their peers were now
worshiping the heavenly bodies they could see, the sun,
moon, and stars. In contrast, Abram looked to God Most
High Creator of heaven and earth, the true God Whom
Noah knew and his sons, Shem Ham and Japheth.
Abram and Sarah were descendants of Shem through
his son, Arphaxad.

Then suddenly had come his life-changing audience
with Him in Whom he trusted, the God of his Fathers,
the one living and true God. God spoke to him. And
the voice of that word, so firm and yet so compassionate,
brought him into the embrace of the fathomless love of

God. To him it was an experience so glorious that his soul became transfixed forever by the wonder of experiencing Reality. And that Reality was the living and true God. Abram knew God was near to him. God had now become the Light of his life. God's love manifested to Abram so filled his soul that he would forever be God's love-bound friend

And now after nearly twenty-five years, of walking in friendship with God, Abraham still trembled to think he could commune with Him face to face, heart to heart. He had also discovered Him to be the One he could most deeply trust, and be most at home with. Of course he felt awe and a holy fear, in the presence of the Almighty who knew him better than he knew himself, yet he had incredible rest in also finding Him to be infinite Love. That day in Ur God had spoken to him saying, :

"Get out of your country
from your kindred
and from your father's house
to a land I will show you.
I will make you a great nation
I will bless you, and you shall be a blessing,
And in you shall all the nations of the earth be
blessed." (Genesis 12:1-3)

Without delay or hesitation, Abraham obeyed God. Thrilled in the marvel of God's great purpose for his life, it was as though he let God take hold of his hand to lead him as a father would his small son.

"For I, the Lord your God, will hold your right hand, saying to you, 'Fear not, I will help you.' (Isaiah 41:13)

This new dimension of faith brought to Abram a new intimacy with God in the wonder of a Divine friendship. Abram felt at home with God.

Hence to live in tents in an alien land had become a sojourn with God who was indeed his Dwelling—place.

And now twenty five years had passed. This warm noonday at Mamre, Abraham's thoughts were contemplating the faithfulness of God. He remembered when he first arrived at Canaan, at Shechem, "And the Canaanites were in the land".(Gen. 12:6)

Abraham was among a foreign people who spoke a language unknown to him. Yet immediately God was there, speaking words of assurance.

"To your descendants I will give this land". (Genesis:12:7)

For Abraham, this promise was of a future time, yet at present he would be a pilgrim, not looking back to return to his home city, but rejoicing in the joy of God's promises. In touch with the living God, Abraham was aware of the inner peace and security of living in His company. At Shechem, he built an altar to the Lord, who had appeared to him there.

As Abraham recalled the many times the Lord had met him and encouraged him through the years of his camping in Canaan, he must have thought often about that very important night when the Lord visited him and cut the Covenant in formal ceremony, making it final. It was on that night that God revealed to Abraham the future of his people. They would be exiled in Egypt for 400 years, after which they would return to Canaan as a nation.

This appearance to him had come the very night after he rescued his nephew, Lot, from the five kings who had captured him in their battle with the kings of Sodom and Gomorrah. With his three hundred and eighteen trained servants, Abraham pursued the enemy as far as Damascus, overcame them, and brought Lot safely back to his home in Sodom.

Abraham must have often wondered about

Melchizedek who came to greet him then, as they were yet in the Valley of Kings, and returning home to Hebron. This man was introduced as Priest of God Most High, and king of Salem. His name, Melchizedek, is interpreted "King of righteousness", and he brought offerings of bread and wine to Abraham, and blessed him, saying:

"Blessed be Abram of God Most High, Possessor of heaven and earth.

And blessed be God Most High Who has delivered your enemies into your hand . . ." (Genesis 14:19,20)

To him Abraham gave deference, and paid him tithes. Nothing more is told of Melchizedek until he is mentioned in Psalm 110, a Messianic prophecy pointing to the eternal priesthood of Messiah. And this reference is also discussed in the New Testament book of Hebrews chapter five.

Back when Abraham was on his way to Hebron after rescuing his nephew, the king of Sodom had met him and offered him gifts of the spoils of war. But Abraham's response to him had been a decided "No".

"I have lifted up my hand to the Lord God Most High, and the Possessor of heaven and earth, that I will take nothing, from a thread to a sandal strap, that I will not take anything that is yours, lest you should say, 'I have made Abraham rich'." (Gen. 14:22,23)

Fourteen years more pilgrimage in Canaan had gone by since this event, and as Abraham recalled it now, he thought of the vision of the Lord that came to him as he slept that night back home in Mamre. The Lord appeared to him, saying,

"Fear not Abram, I am your Shield, and your exceedingly great Reward". Abraham had answered Him, opening his heart as to a dearest friend,

"Lord, what will You give me seeing I go childless. And the heir of my house is Eliezar of Damascus?"

God's answer was His promise that the heir to the Covenant would be his very own son. (Genesis 17)

Here the tryst with God becomes intimate and near,

"He brought him outside, and said, 'Look now toward heaven and count the stars if you are able to number them. So shall your descendants be'." (Genesis 15)

Abraham listened to Him Who is Truth itself confiding in him. And he trusted Him with all his soul, appropriating God into his life more deeply than ever. Faith is transforming because faith obeys God in the ability that God supplies him to do so. Receiving His strength to obey Him, we partake of Him.

"God is the Strength of my life." Says the psalmist often.

And, for Abraham, the friend of God forever, obedience is always motivated by genuine love for Him—the deep affection of adoration and worship. Worship sets God on the throne in our hearts.

Abraham's believing God is reckoned unto him for righteousness. This is not merely imputed righteousness because faith accesses the mighty power of the Spirit of God which can work in us that evidence of Himself in us that pleases and glorifies God. To quote Dr. Robertson McQuilkin :

"Glorifying God should stem out of sincere and deep love for Him. Man's chief end is to love the Lord with all his heart, soul, and mind. One way to express that love is to glorify Him, to put the spotlight on His glorious character." (from the summer issue of Connection, CIU '01)

The New Testament book of Galatians refers to the Abrahamic Covenant as a way in which the scriptures "preached the Gospel to Abraham. saying, 'In you all nations shall be blessed' . . . Now to Abraham and to his Seed were the promises made. He does not say, 'And to seeds, as of many, but as one, 'And to your Seed' which is Christ'." (Gal. 3:8 &16)

In this light, it is wonderful to realize that the centerpiece of God's Covenant of Grace is the Incarnation, the greatest truth of all Time. It is the Fact of history that pivots the calendar from BC to AD, and tells of Bethlehem, Calvary, Resurrection, and future Hope

Our priority petition to our Father in heaven is, "Thy kingdom come, Thy will be done on earth as it is in Heaven."

For all the years that Abraham had sojourned in Canaan, building an altar at every milestone, and living a nomadic life in temporary tents, he never looked back or thought of returning to Chaldea (Iraq), but rather, he lived in friendship with the living God. He looked forward to "a City, which has foundation, whose builder and maker was God". (Hebrews 11:10)

The altars of Abraham in Canaan were sign posts to "The City of God". He walked in contrast to the peoples around him, yet they witnessed his life, that God was with him, and he seemed to them "A mighty Prince among us". (Genesis 23:6)

"What is the righteousness which is by faith? It is simply the thing that God wants every man to be, wrought out in him by constant obedient contact with God Himself. It is God's righteousness wrought out in us so that as He is righteous we too are righteous." (George MacDonald "Discovering the Character of God" by Michael Phillips Bethany House Publishers)

This day in his old age as Abraham sat at his tent door in Mamre, lost in thought, he felt strangely stirred. Excited. God had just appeared to him two evenings ago. His coming had been to Abraham a new fresh revelation of Himself. He appeared to him and said,

"I am Almighty God, El Shaddai,". To interpret, He is the God who is enough, sufficient, all you need. "Walk before Me and be blameless. And I will make My Covenant with you, and will multiply you exceedingly."

This was the night God had given him the name Abraham instead of Abram. The new name meant "Father of a multitude." As he sensed the immediate, almost tangible presence of the Almighty, Abraham had fallen on his face in worship as God spoke with him.

Suddenly a fresh hope quickened his spirit. That same promise had come again, despite the fact that he now had his son Ishmael by Sarah's maid, Hagar. But God had another plan in mind. The faith of Abraham at this hour is expressed well in Phillip's translation of Romans 4:18-21:

"Abraham, when hope was dead within him, went on hoping in faith, believing that he would become 'the father of many nations'. He relied upon the word of God which definitely referred to "thy Seed". With undaunted faith he looked at the facts—his own impotence (he was practically a hundred years old at the time) and his wife Sarah's apparent barrenness, yet he refused to allow any distrust of a definite pronouncement of God to make him waver. He drew strength from his faith, and while giving the glory to God, remained absolutely convinced that God was able to implement His own promise. This was the faith "which was counted unto him for righteousness.'"

At this hour with God, Abraham was instructed to institute the rite of circumcision, as a sign of the final seal of the Covenant. And Abraham had obeyed and carried out those instructions "that very same day".(Genesis 17)

Sitting in the sparse shade of terebinths around noon, Abraham kept his thoughts upon El Shaddai, a name he found most comforting, a new insight into the Person he loved and worshiped. He was eager always to grow in the knowledge of Him.

Suddenly he became aware of unexpected company. Raising his eyes, he was startled to see Angelic guests before him, standing under the trees. He thought perhaps they were intending to go on their way somewhere else, so he ran to welcome them, begging them to stay for dinner. But they had indeed come with astounding news.

"Then they said to him," reads the account in Genesis,

'Where is Sarah your wife?' And he said,

'Here in the tent'."

The One of the three angels that Abraham addressed as the Angel of the Lord said to him,

"I will certainly return to you according to the time of life, and Sarah your wife shall have a son." (Genesis 18:9,10)

These amazing words were greeted with laughter, at first of incredulity, and then of faith. For the Lord had just uttered the question, charged with power and glory,

"Is anything too hard for the Lord?"(Genesis 18:14)

"Faith mighty faith
The promise sees and looks to God alone,
Laughs at impossibilities and cries "It shall be done".
(Charles Wesley)

"By faith Sarah herself also received strength to conceive seed, and she bore a child when she was past age, because she judged Him faithful Who had promised." (Heb. 11:11)

So it was within the next year when Abraham was one hundred years old, and Sarah in her nineties, that

Isaac, their son, was born. Isaac means "Laughter". And in the tents of Abraham there was gladness and laughter, and Sarah said,

"God has made me laugh so all who hear will laugh with me."

God had given the son of promise, an heir to the Covenant which foretold the Seed of Abraham would one day come to earth,

"The Seed which is Christ, that the blessing of Abraham might come upon the Gentiles in Christ Jesus."

We might wonder how much did Abraham perceive that this promise of the Messiah, the Christ was the definitive core prophecy of God's Covenant with him? It was the Covenant made by God in Trinity (Genesis 15), and was named an Everlasting Covenant. We note that it was the Lord Himself, in speaking to the Pharisees and Rulers, who said to them,

"Your Father Abraham rejoiced to see My Day, and he saw it and was glad." (John 8:56).

In this same passage in the Gospel of John, Jesus had made another startling statement. "Jesus said to them,

'Most assuredly, I say to you, before Abraham *was*, I Am.'" (John 8:58).

We may ponder the truth that The Angel of the Lord whom Abraham would meet again and again, to talk with him in his long sojourn in Canaan, was the very Person speaking to His people that day in Jerusalem,

"Whose goings forth have been of old, even from everlasting." (Micah 5:2)

For the Covenant of Grace He established for Abraham and his progeny held within its essential purpose the redemption of the world.

"For God so loved the world that He gave His only

begotten Son that whoever believes in Him shall not perish but have everlasting life." (John 3:16)

And God told Abraham that in Isaac his Seed would be called. Now the heir to the Covenant has come. At last Abraham and Sarah know the joy of fulfilled hope. Their faith is reinforced in witnessing again that "nothing is too hard for the Lord,"

Isaac is the new link in the chain that binds the descendants of Abraham to a promised One, the Messiah, that is, the Christ of God.

The One among his Angel visitors that Abraham addressed as the Lord was indeed the Theophany, or appearance to him of that One, the second Person of the Trinity, whom the apostle John refers to as the Word.

"And the Word was made flesh and dwelt among us, and we beheld His glory, the glory as of the only begotten of the Father, full of grace and truth." (John 1:14)

The Angel of the Lord had promised Isaac. And now the heir to the Everlasting Covenant gladdened the lives of his parents, and Abraham the friend of God believed.

Could he have comprehended the amazing fact that one day this very One would Himself fulfill His date in human history, and, at cost beyond our understanding, insure redemption for each person who will choose to receive Him as did Abraham? Of Him, risen from the Dead, the the Gospel of Luke says,

"And beginning at Moses (Genesis), and all the Prophets, He expounded to them in all the scriptures the things concerning Himself." (Luke 24:27)

As the biography of Abraham continues, we will next center our thoughts on his son, Isaac, the heir to the Covenant.

# Called Unto Friendship

Abram found himself to be
In audience with Deity.
He heard in words that awesome voice
How could he then make other choice
Than welcome Him to trust, obey.
No other plan, no other way

What secret place so safe and best,
Than in the Most High find his rest?
Unfathomed Love, eternal Hope
The City of God, his glorious scope.
The temporal dimmed as Abraham found
His walk with God on holy ground.

The will of God he made his will,
Knowing His word He would fulfill,.
His lasting Covenant unfold
That greatest story ever told.
The Seed of Abraham, Christ of God
Would walk these paths God's friend had trod.

# Chapter Eight

## Heir to the Covenant

"In knowing God is Life and its gladness"
George MacDonald

"Though He slay me, yet will I trust Him" was the cry of faith spoken by Job. And in the life of seventeen year old Isaac these words were to be silently enacted at Moriah. That mountain, Moriah, would mean to Abraham the deepest testing of his faith, and to Isaac his own discovery of God.

At this time the family of Abraham lived at Beersheba, the place that means "the well of the oath". The nearby Philistines had at last promised not to contest this well, but to concede it to Abraham who had dug it. There Abraham planted a tamarisk tree as a further reminder of this agreement. And there he "called on the name of the Lord, the Everlasting God." (Genesis 21:33)

The Name of God is the sum of all He is in all His attributes, and the many aspects of His Being that speak to His relationship with His own creation, and with His own people.

Sometime after this God spoke to Abraham one night, and said,

"Abraham,", and Abraham answered,

"Here I am". And God, testing him, said.

"Take now your son, your only son Isaac, whom you love, and go to the land of Moriah, and offer him there as a burnt offering on one of the mountains of which I shall tell you." (Gen. 22:1,2)

At this moment Abraham was given in profound heart-searching, both Gethsemane and Calvary to taste of in anguish. Yet he was steadfast in his choice. Though shaken to the depths in his spirit, Abraham could only answer God's command with a decision that said to Him,

"Not my will, but Yours be done". (Luke 22:42)

With Abraham, there was no alternative to God's revealed will. The consequence of obedience must be left to God also. For with Abraham, God was his very Life.

We might expect this to be true of "the friend of God forever", but that it was also true of his teenage Isaac is a marvel here, that is, Isaac's unflinching submission to his father, as well as to the God of his father Whom he would soon behold for himself with unforgettable clarity . . .

"So Abraham rose early in the morning and saddled his donkey, and took two of his young men with him, and Isaac his son; and he split wood for the burnt offering and arose and went to the place of which God had told him. Then on the third day Abraham lifted up his eyes and saw the place afar off." (Genesis 22:3, 4)

"Stay here with the donkey." he instructed the young men,

"The lad and I will go yonder and worship, and we will come back to you." (Gen.22:5)

In the unexplained mystery of God's request at this time, Abraham knew in the depths of his spirit that Isaac was still the essential link in the fulfillment of that great Covenant. Therefore he believed that the two of them would most certainly return. How, he could not imagine.

He had said nothing to Isaac about the purpose behind this trip to Moriah. But when he took the wood of the burnt offering and laid it upon Isaac's shoulders, and he took the fire in his hand and a knife, as the two of them began to ascend the mountain together, Isaac quietly asked a pertinent question,

"My Father", and he said

"Here I am, my son".

"Look, the fire and the wood, but where is the lamb for the burnt offering?

"And Abraham said, 'the Lord will provide Himself a lamb for the burnt offering'. And the two of them went together." (Gen.22:7,8)

Both father and son were involved in this sacred consecration offering. Working against his surging emotions and his great love for his only beloved child given at last to himself and Sarah, Abraham, in the power of an even greater affection and devotion began with Isaac to build that terrible altar on Mount Moriah. When the altar was ready, Abraham silently laid the wood on the altar. He then laid Isaac upon the wood, binding him there to the altar.

Isaac made no protest, uttered not a word. Perhaps he kept his eyes open, looking up into the sky, remembering his trusted father's assurance that God would provide the lamb for the burnt offering. He saw his father's arm raised with the knife flashing in the sun. Then suddenly came a rift in near heaven, and Isaac could look up into the face of the Lord, his first personal contact with the living God!

The Angel of the Lord called from heaven,

"Abraham, Abraham!" And he said,

"Here I am." And He said

"Do not lay your hand upon the lad, or do anything to him for now I know that you fear God for you have not withheld your son, your only son, from Me." Gen. 22:11,12)

Immediately Abraham lifted up his eyes to see a ram caught by its horns in a thicket. This was God's provision for the burnt offering. How joyfully then, with trembling hands Abraham used the knife to cut away the bonds from his son, Isaac.

How profound and life changing was Isaac's beholding the God of his father Abraham. He knew Him here on Moriah as his own Jehovah-Jirah . . . Young Isaac trembled in His presence.

At this place, both Isaac and his father found :

"that fear almost stood before strength, that the visible God is the destruction of death, . . . that the one and only safety in the universe is the perfect nearness of the Living One. *God is Being, Death is nowhere.*" (George MacDonald "Discovering the Character of God" p 98)

Isaac stood with his father at the altar worshiping God. Together they had just discovered this new meaning of the Name of God. His Name is Jehovah-Jirah, the ever present God, "I Am Who provides."

He indeed provided the sacrifice on the altar at Mount Moriah. In centuries future this spot would become the site of the Temple in Jerusalem which in every part speaks the character and work of Messiah, the promised Seed of Abraham and Isaac.

"And Abraham called the name of the place," The Lord will provide, as it is said unto this day, 'In the Mount of the Lord it shall be provided.' (Gen. 22:14)".

Before Isaac and his father left the mountain to return to the young men as they had promised, Isaac was to experience a second revelation of God, and the words he heard he could never forget. He would often recall them and meditate upon them, and teach them to his children.

"Then the Angel of the Lord called to Abraham a second time out of heaven, and said,

'By Myself I have sworn, says the Lord, because you have done this thing, and have not withheld your son, your only son, in blessing I will bless you, and in multiplying I will multiply your descendants as the stars of the heaven, and as the sand which is on the seashore, and your descendants shall possess the gate of their enemies.

In your Seed all the nations of the earth shall be blessed, because you have obeyed My voice." (Gen. 22 : 15-17).

It is this passage from the biography of Abraham that James recalls in his assertion that "Faith without works is dead." In other words, the faith of Abraham acted in obedience, which deed evidenced the genuineness of his faith. In this context, James quotes the great cornerstone of Abraham's life.

"Abraham believed God, and it was accounted to him for righteousness." And James adds,

"And he was called the friend of God."

This story of Abraham and Isaac is a graphic picture of that scene of Christ crucified, of God in Christ reconciling the world unto Himself at Calvary, then, after three days, raising Him from the Dead.

"By faith Abraham, when he was tested, offered up Isaac, and he, who had received the promises offered up his only son, of whom it was said, 'In Isaac your Seed shall be called,' accounting that God was able to raise him up, even from the dead from which he also received him, *in a figurative sense*." (Hebrews 11:17-19)

In this climactic test of the faith of Abraham, we discover that in his life with God, God's gift of Isaac, his beloved son, had in no way rivaled Abraham's devotion to His God. God remained the Joy of all his joys, the first in all the precious gifts from His hand. His son Isaac, dear as he was, could not displace God

Himself from the center and the circumference of his
soul.

This tells us that the gifts God bestows upon us are
best enjoyed when kept within our priority relationship
with God Himself. Kept in God, they are permanent. In
God they enhance our love and gratitude to Him. We
are admonished to keep ourselves from idols. This
Abraham indeed had done. And the heart of God
rejoiced that it was so.

For Isaac, heir to the Covenant of God's Grace, this
unforgettable introduction to the God of Glory, the
*present* Jehovah-Jirah would be the foundation of his
own personal faith in God, and of his walk with Him . . .
He would be aware always of the great calling of his
people to magnify the Name of the Lord in witness to
all nations of the living and true Creator, Possessor of
heaven and earth.

The next great event in Isaac's life was the death of
his mother, Sarah, whom he loved so deeply . . . Her
death at one hundred and twenty-seven years occurred
in Isaac's early thirties. At this time, Abraham purchased
the only piece of land his people owned in Canaan for
hundreds of years. He bought the deed from the Hittites
at Hebron at four hundred silver shekels, and thereby
possessed the Cave and Field of Machpelah, the burial
ground for his family. The dead were buried there after
they had been "gathered up". This phrase seems to be
the equivalent of saying, "with the Lord". The idea is
that of being joined again to their own people in "the
age to come" to use the phrase Christ expressed on this
subject. Job also refers to this idiom when he speaks of
the wicked who "lie down, but are not gathered up."
(Job 27:19)

In Matthew, Mark and Luke we have parallel verses

which record a conversation Jesus had with the Sadducees. They had asked a complicated question about heaven, to which Jesus replied, knowing that the Sadducees did not believe in heaven or angels or resurrection life, and He told them,

"You are mistaken, not knowing the Scriptures nor the power of God . . . Have you not read what was spoken to you by God, saying, I am the God of Abraham, the God of Isaac, and the God of Jacob'? God is not the God of the dead but of the living." (Matt. 22:29-32; Mark 12 24-27; Luke. 20:34-38)

Hebrews chapter eleven brings us the vision of what Abraham, Isaac, and Jacob were assured of by faith:

"These all died in faith, not having received the promises, but having seen them afar off were assured of them, embraced them, and confessed that they were strangers and pilgrims on earth. . . . . But now they desire a better, that is, a heavenly country. Therefore God is not ashamed to be called their God, for He has prepared a city for them." (Hebrews 11: 13,16)

"Death is a beginning, not an end. The darkness falls, and in the sky is a distant glow, the lights of . . . the City of God Looking toward them, I say over to myself John Donne's splendid words: "Death, thou shalt die." In the graveyard, the dust settles; in the City of God, eternity begins." (Malcolm Muggeridge, Twentieth Century Testimony by Thomas Howard)

Isaac was now forty years old when the beautiful twenty-fourth chapter of Genesis relates the romantic story of finding a bride for him. In exquisite literary form the story of how Abraham's trusted servant, ruler of all his house, is sent to find a bride for Isaac. She must come from Abraham's own kindred in Haran. To encourage his eldest servant in this challenge, Abraham, assures him that

"the Lord God of Heaven . . . will send His angel before you."

The servant solemnly vowed to go on the long journey north to Mesopotamia to the city of Nahor. Taking with him ten camels and servants and many costly gifts, he went trusting in the God of his Master Abraham. The quest was an exciting success, as the servant told of it,

"I, being on the way, the Lord led me". (Genesis 24: 27)

At the well in the outskirts of Nahor, the very first person he met was the beautiful maiden, Rebekah. She was the right person of the right family, and they were all aware of God's leading.


Rebekah consented to go to Canaan with the kind old servant, head of the house of Abraham.

Meanwhile, Isaac, who lived in the South, had gone out to meditate in the field in the evening. What prayer thoughts must have been his? "The God Who Sees" was the place-name where his tents were pitched. In his language, it was called Beer Lahai Roi. Isaac knew God was always near, and he loved and worshiped Him in utmost trust. While in the field at dusk, Isaac lifted up his eyes and behold, there came the camel train of his father!

At the same time, Rebekah saw him, and finding out he was Isaac, she dismounted her camel, put a veil over her face, and walked to meet Isaac, along with the servant who introduced them to each other. Isaac took her to his mother's tent that night, and their marriage, thus "made in heaven" was one of love and joy. Isaac was then comforted in the loss of his mother, Sarah.

Isaac and Rebekah lived in Beer Lahai Roi. After twenty years when Isaac was sixty years old, and his father Abraham was yet alive, Isaac and Rebekah still had no children. Isaac believed God's Covenant purpose for his people, yet he must face the fact that they had no son to inherit those promises made to Abraham, and to himself. As he, like his father, walked daily "before the Lord", Isaac came to Him one day with a definite and urgent prayer.

"Now Isaac pleaded with the Lord for his wife because she was barren, and the Lord granted his plea." (Gen. 25:21)

At last twin sons were born to Isaac and Rebekah, Esau and Jacob. The children were almost whimsically named. Esau was hairy and red, so he obtained the name meaning *red*, and Jacob whose hand held on to his brother's heel was called Jacob meaning *supplanter.*

At this time Isaac and Rebekah were told that it would be Jacob who would inherit the Covenant. Despite his faults in living up to his name often, it was Jacob who would be drawn to reverence and obey God. In contrast, Esau, who, though attractive and popular, never showed an interest in the eternal things of God.

In observing Isaac's walk with God, we have a profile of his life and character in Genesis 26:11-33. The witness of Isaac was in his actions rather than in words. His gentle example spoke the beauty of a "meek and quiet spirit". In fact, "in the beauty of holiness" he lived among his sometimes hostile neighbors. The fact that God had blessed and made him so prosperous, "for he had possessions of flocks and possessions of herds, and a great number of servants," caused the Philistines to envy him. (Gen. 26:14)

"Then Abimelech, a title meaning King, said to Isaac,
'Go away from us for you are mightier than we.'" (Gen. 26:16)

Then meekly, Isaac, with all his household and possessions, moved away, and pitched his tents in the Valley of Gerar, and began to settle down there. He found that the Philistines had stopped up the wells that his father Abraham had dug,so he had his servants restore them. But as soon as Isaac's servants found running water in the well in Gerar, herdsmen of the Philistines came in to challenge and quarrel with his men. When they claimed the well to be theirs, Isaac packed up his tents and moved on. This he did silently without protest. He named that well *Esek*, or strife.

Again, Isaac found another well the neighbors had stopped up. And his servants dug and restored it. They found there was water enough, so Isaac again set up his tents to stay awhile. But presently the Philistine herdsmen came again and in much anger, they demanded this well too. Without a rebuke, Isaac broke camp once more, and journeyed on.

He named that well also calling it *Sitnah* which means enmity. It is interesting that the sound of the word, *Sitnah*, is like the hiss of a serpent. But Isaac remained a gentleman, and was kind and even joyful in his manner before his enemies. In this way he proved to the people around him that his resources of heart and soul were the deep eternal wells of life communing with the living God. Isaac's walk with God is not dramatic, but genuine in the hidden strength found in meditating on God, keeping in touch with Him through prayer. It was George Buttrick who said,

"*Prayer is friendship with God.*" (George Buttrick-1895-1980 from Devotional Classics, edited by John Foster and James Bryan

Smith, Hoddard and Stoughton, London)

In a sense it seems that Isaac mirrors the nature of God in reflecting the God of Glory to his neighbors. Isaac reminds us again of the statement that

"Man's chief end is to glorify God, and to enjoy Him forever."

To Isaac this was the secret of peace and contentment within a hostile environment, and in his experiences of adversity.

"A man's vision in the things of God can be trusted only to the extent that man is himself walking with God" (George MacDonald "Discovering the Character of God" p129 by Michael Phillips)

Isaac moved another time and came to a dry well. There his servants dug again and found water. But at this place there was no contesting of the well. Isaac exclaimed,

"Now the Lord has made room for us, and we shall be fruitful in the land." And he named the place *Rohoboth* which means *room*. (Gen. 26:22)

Later, Isaac went up from Rohoboth to Beersheba, and "The Lord appeared to him the same night, and said,

"I am the God of your father Abraham, do not fear, for I am with you. I will bless you, and multiply your descendants for My servant Abraham's sake."

"So he built an altar there, and called on the name of the Lord." (Genesis 26:24,25)

Here Isaac marked the milestone of his pilgrimage with the altar, the Old Testament symbol of the Cross.

Just as his servants were digging the well at Beersheba and finding abundant water, unexpected guests from the Philistines appeared before Isaac again. And Isaac said to them,

"Why have you come to me since you hate me and have sent me away from you?" He was addressing the King, entitled Abimelech, with his friend, Ahuzzah, and Phichol, the captain of his army. But they said,

"We have certainly seen that the Lord is with you . . . . You are now the blessed of the Lord."

Isaac then made a feast for them, and they stayed overnight.

"Then they arose early in the morning, and swore an oath with one another, and Isaac sent them away, and they departed from him in peace." (Genesis 26:27-33)

"And it came to pass the same day that Isaac's servants came and told him about the well which they had dug, and said to him,

"We have found water." So Isaac called it Sheba, which means "seven" or "an oath". So it was that Beershebah, the well of the oath, often became the dwelling place of Isaac and his family.

Isaac, in his mild and pleasant tenor and gentle witness in his walk with God, is not the vivid, unforgettable personality his father Abraham was, nor as Jacob would be who is the next heir to the Covenant. Isaac is almost a mere conjunction between his father and his son. Yet with thoughtful observation of his portrait in Genesis, Isaac appears as those of whom the Psalmist writes,

"They looked unto Him, and were radiant, and their faces were not ashamed."(Psalm 34:5)

He is like the blessed Man of Psalm One who walks not in the counsel of the ungodly. He delights in meditating on God, and in doing His pleasure, His will. He is like a tree planted beside the wells of water. Quietly the life of God in him is verdant and fruitful. And whatever he does is prospering. Isaac is the individual God designed him to be.

"For the Lord knows the way of the righteous."

The miracle son of Abraham and Sarah lived out his unquestioning trust in his father's God with such reverence and awe that the scriptures speak of the God of Abraham, and the *Fear* of Isaac. Thus the word Fear is a term for Deity that identifies the reverential quality of Isaac's faith, and walk with God.

He recalls the God who provides at the altar the sacrifice for his life, and the God of that awesome Covenant that foretells the Savior of the world.

Walking in the beauty of humility and trust, Isaac is the rightful heir to God's promises given his father Abraham.

"You will keep him in perfect peace whose mind is stayed on You because he trusts in You. For in Jehovah, the Lord, is everlasting strength." (Isaiah 26: 3,4)

# Truth Spoke the Word

Thou understandeth well our frame, dear Lord.
Thou knowest too that we were made of dust.
Then my Savior answered; Truth spoke the word
The earthen vessel crumbles as it must.

Within it is the person that thou art.
I am thy Source and thine expected Goal.
I set eternity within thy heart.
Dust and ashes free thy heaven-bound soul.
Thy pilgrimage on earth is a known way,
For it is my own loving plan for thee.
Its end begins thine everlasting Day.
That where I am there also thou shalt be.

Lord, be Thou now my Dwelling-place, I said.
Thou God of Peace, of Hope, of saving Grace.
My Home, my Peace, my Hope, my daily Bread.
Until that Morning shines upon Thy Face.

# Chapter Nine

## Prince with God

"And I will write on him My new Name."
(Rev. 3:29)

Jacob stood on a stony piece of ground where terebinth trees gradually darkened into solid shadows. The sun had already set. He watched the final embers of a day that had passed, as the night spread over him, a solitary man, clothed in a shepherd's attire, holding his shepherd's staff in his hand, all that he now owned.

At this crisis in his life, Jacob had been uprooted from the life he had known throughout his forty years, days of pastoral peace and harmony in his godly home, his familiar surroundings. These had suddenly been torn away . . . Today he was in flight upon a long journey northward to Haran in Syria where his mother's people lived.

What would his future be? He wondered. Isaac, his father, had given him the blessing of God, and both parents firmly admonished their younger son to never marry a daughter of the Canaanites. He must take a wife of the daughters of his mother's people instead. The wives their son Esau had married of the daughters of Heth had brought much grief and disappointment to Isaac and Rebekah. So Jacob promised to obey them in this important matter and to return to them again in Canaan.

Tonight the burden of this separation was heavy. He realized that his father was already one hundred years old, and blind. Would he ever see him again on earth? Rebekah, who was also his closest friend and confidant, was in her eightieth year by now. And, as the story of Jacob's life is given us in Genesis, his mother would not live to see Jacob again. However, it was the wrath of Esau toward him that precipitated Jacob's present flight to Padan Aram, and the city of Haran, home of his mother's brother, Laban. This evening at the end of a strenuous march northward, his heart was grieving over what he had done to alienate his brother, Esau. He kept hearing his brother's strident voice even now, crying out,

"Is he not rightly named Jacob? For he has supplanted me these two times!"

Esau spoke the truth. Jacob had again, along with the scheming of his mother, lived up to his name, *Jacob*, which means deceiver, or supplanter. The result was Jacob's deceiving his father into giving him the blessing of the firstborn son. Almost catching Jacob in the act of impersonating him, Esau became furious. He was overheard even threatening the life of his brother.

Now Jacob's very soul was battered by those unforgiving words,

"Is he not rightly named *Jacob*?" And finally, "I will kill my brother!"

Certainly here at Luz Jacob felt destitute. Alone. Yet it is at this low point of his desperate need, that God takes the initiative. Since Jacob's first step of personal faith must be his own personal understanding of God, and not just following the tradition of his Fathers, God Himself, the God of Jacob, draws near and reveals Himself to him.

This night Jacob is humbled. He is contrite, and "poor in spirit", needing deeply to find God for himself. I think of how Jacob fits the first Beatitude here:

"Blessed are the poor in spirit, for *theirs is the Kingdom of heaven*." (Matt. 5:1)

Weary and discouraged, Jacob looked around and found a stone he could use for a pillow, and he lay down exhausted and fell asleep. As he slept, he dreamed of a ladder set on earth reaching up to the very gates of Glory and to God Himself. This stairway to heaven was crowded with angels ascending and descending upon it. The dream continued with the very voice of the Most High, who stood at the top of the ladder, repeating to Jacob that great promise of the Abrahamic Covenant, that

"In you and in your seed all the families of the earth shall be blessed." (Genesis 28:13)

"Behold I am with you wherever you go, and will bring you back to this land, for I will not leave you until I have done what I have spoken to you."

"Then Jacob awoke from his sleep and said, 'Surely the Lord was in this place and I did not know it!'" (Gen. 28:15,16)

And he was afraid and said, 'How awesome is this place! This is none other than the House of God, and this if the gate of heaven!'" (Genesis 28: 15-17)

At that early morning hour, Jacob, still trembling in awe of his first revelation of God, took the stone which had been his pillow, and poured oil upon it. With this marker, Jacob named the place *Bethel* which means the *House of God*.

Then Jacob, in solemn awareness of God's nearness, made a vow to Him. He spoke in the hush of this astounding vision. For he had both seen God standing at the open gate of heaven, and heard His voice bequeathing to him, Jacob, those words of promise that both Abraham and Isaac had received from Him.

After this person to person experience of the God of his Fathers, Jacob would never be the same, although he had always desired and held dear to his heart the things of God. The Divine purposes shown to his Fathers had always been important to Jacob, and he had reverenced the God of Abraham and Isaac.

In this he was a contrast to Esau who is called a profane man Esau enjoyed God's blessings, however God Himself had no place in his thoughts. It was Jacob, who welcomed God into his life with genuine desire toward Him. Hence, finding God for himself in such a real discovery of His true Being, would begin for Jacob a decided change in his personality and character. The process had now begun that would see him transformed from *Jacob* to *Israel*. From this moment on he would grow in his relationship with God.

The story of Jacob shows us the God of Jacob. It enriches the significance of the poet's words,:

"Happy is he who makes the God of Jacob his Refuge". (Psalm 46:7)

Malcolm Muggeridge, on the subject of God revealing Himself to a person, says,

"From such an encounter with God, what emerges? That we are indeed made in His image, and, though fallen creatures and inheritors of Adam's curse, we may aspire to participate in His purposes . . . Nevertheless, knowing God brings with it the requisite faith to surrender wholly to His purposes." (Twentieth Century Testimony, by Thomas Howard)

Even with his first earnest resolves before God, Jacob was already a new person for he had found in God the forgiveness and mercy which brought inner peace to his soul. Now Jacob begins speaking his thoughts, still marveling at God's grace toward him.

"If God will be with me, and keep me in this way that I am going, and give me bread to eat and clothing to put on so that I come back to my father's house in peace, then the Lord shall be my God." (Gen. 28:21)

The emphasis in his heart here is the amazing aspect of God's kindness lifting *Jacob* to the the status known by his grandfather Abraham, who is called the "Friend of God", and to that of Isaac who also walked with God. Jacob continues in addressing God directly, "And this stone which I have set as a pillar shall be God's house, and of all that You give me I will surely give a tenth to you." (Gen. 28:22)

The tithe is first mentioned when Abraham paid tithes to Melchizedek, a priest of the Most High God, when he blessed Abraham after the victory over the five kings who had abducted his nephew Lot. To this priest, Abraham's tithe acknowledged God as the One who had given him this victory. The tithe is a symbolic confession that God Himself is our Source of all blessing. A tithe of what is already His own links us to Him openly. We do not forget to Whom we belong. Giving back to Him is recognizing His priority in our lives.

This very first personal meeting with the living God is revoltionary for Jacob. Though his name was *Jacob*, it would, in time, become *Israel, a Prince with God.* For the story of Jacob is the saga of a flawed life transformed by God's grace into a life ennobled and made new. God would do this for Jacob by His wisdom and by the continuing revelation of Himself all along his pilgrimage . . .

It is the Prophet, Isaiah who unveils to us in words God's, side of the story of Jacob. He articulates the compassion and intimacy of the love of God for Jacob and his descendants:

"But you, Israel, are my servant, Jacob, whom I have

chosen, the descendants of Abraham My friend . . . . I have chosen you, and have not cast you away.

Fear not, for I am with you; Be not dismayed, for I am your God.

I will strengthen you, Yes, I will help you, I will uphold you with My righteous right hand.

For I, the Lord your God, will hold your right hand, saying unto you, 'Fear not, I will help you.'" (Isaiah 41:8-10; 13)

God's revealing Himself to Jacob made Bethel not only the place where Jacob first began to know and walk with God, but also where God showed him the way to His Kingdom. The ladder accessing heaven was *set on earth*. At other times Jacob will return to Bethel. It would always signify the place of beginnings to him. And there he must first build the altar in preparing to meet with God. The altar with its sin-offering is where that access to communing with God is first established. The Lamb slain is the threshold always for us who enter into the presence of God, as those who belong in His House.

"Behold! The Lamb of God Who takes away the sin of the world.", said John, in introducing Christ Jesus to his own disciples. The Gospel according to John chapter one records this statement twice.

From before the foundation of the world, the sacrifice of the Lamb of God, is the place of our access to God. That the altar of sacrifice for sin is essential for communion with God is clear throughout all the scriptures. His truth is the same in every generation. One altar, that is, One cross. One Sacrifice. The ladder is the same. One ladder. It is definitive that Christ identified Himself with this ladder in this same context in John's Gospel.

"Jesus saw Nathaniel coming toward Him and said,
'Behold an Israelite in whom is no 'guile (no *Jacob*)!'

"Nathaniel said to Him, 'How do you know me?'
Jesus answered and said to him,

'Before Philip called you, when you were under the
fig tree, I saw you.'

"Nathaniel answered and said unto Him,

'Rabbi, You are the Son of God! You are the King of
Israel!' Jesus answered and said to him,


'Because I said to you, "I saw you under the fig tree",
do you believe? You will see greater things than
these.' . . . "Most assuredly, I say to you,

'Hereafter you shall see heaven open, and the angels
of God ascending and descending upon the Son of
Man.'" (John 1: 47-51)

The Seed of Abraham. Isaac and Jacob is that very
Christ, the Son of Man.

The Truth of God stands timeless in the decrees of
God. It is future fact in Jacob's day, and historical fact in
ours, yet unchanging and efficacious unto all
generations.

Access to God through Christ brings us to enjoy the
gifts of heaven. The traffic of angels tells of God's
blessings to us from heaven.

So it is that Jacob, having nothing, as he heads toward
Haran, is yet the recipient of abundant resources. He
walks with God. He has access to Him. Angels minister
unto him.

Since obedience to God is the outward effect of
faith, and the inward truth of walking with Him, we
see how the transformed life works. We can observe
how the ways of Jacob are exchanged for the ways of
God. We discover that obedience can be motivated,
not by a sense of duty that we struggle to do in our

own effort, but by worship, by choosing, above all
else, to please Him.

How applicable to the youth, Jacob, as to everyone,
is the principle stated in the book of Proverbs. (Proverbs
3:5,6)

"Trust in the Lord with all your heart,

And lean not on your own understanding.

In all your ways acknowledge Him,

And He shall direct your paths."

Again let us hear Isaiah's glimpse into the Heart of
God, of His initiative in Redemption:

"But now, thus says the Lord, who created you, O
Jacob, and He who formed you, O Israel. 'Fear not, for I
have redeemed you, I have called you by your name.
You are mine.'" (Isaiah 43:1)

As Jacob went on his journey and finally came to
the land of the people of the East, he walked with a
new joy. God had a great purpose for his life. And he
knew that God was with him. He now could be set free
from anxiety. Still needy, he now realized his adequate
Resource in his God, near, intimate, caring.

So it was that at his very first approach to his Uncles'
place at Haran, God opened hospitable doors to Jacob,
Rebekah's son. Almost immediately, God gave him
Rachael whom he loved devotedly, and Jacob agreed
with Laban to work seven years to obtain her at last as
his bride.

"So Jacob served seven years for Rachael, and they
seemed but a few days to him because of the love he
had for her." (Genesis 29:30)

However, Jacob's years at Haran would be not only
joy and good fortune, a large family, and much gain in
livestock and material prosperity, for God was with him
indeed.

But hard lessons were to come too. Laban seemingly
kept his word. After Jacob's seven years of labor, his

wedding day finally came. He and his veiled Bride were married.

But, the next morning, Jacob saw that his Uncle had given him Rachael's older sister Leah to wed. Shocked and dismayed at such deception, Jacob rushed to his Uncle to protest. Laban calmly stated to him that their custom forbid marrying off the younger before the older daughter. He then promised Rachael to him as well, after one week. However, Jacob had to work another seven years for this solution. These would be only the beginnings of Jacob's trials with his Uncles' deceptive ways.

It is notable how God has built into the laws of life a predictable principle. It is known as the law of retribution, the principle of sowing and reaping.

"Whatsoever a man sows that shall he also reap". "If we sow the wind, we reap the whirlwind" (Gal. 6:7; Hosea 8:7)

This correction designed by our Creator, our heavenly Father, shows us plainly how much better it is to "walk in paths of righteousness for His Name's sake". (Psalm 23:3)

It is seen in Jacob's life again and again that because he had sown deceit, though forgiven, he often suffered from the deception of others, of his Uncle Laban, and even of his own elder sons. God thus uses hardship and adversity, and sometimes anguish and sorrow, to mellow and correct, and to solidify Jacob's resolve to walk with God. This fact is, as by default, the experience common to mankind.

It is exciting in reading this narrative as Genesis records it, that at every turning in the road, at every lurking peril, every test, the God of Jacob is there for Jacob. And like Abraham and Isaac, Jacob too, gratefully and eagerly responded to His voice in unquestioning obedience.

Always, it is God Himself within His gifts and blessings, that is by far the greatest gift of all. Every good gift becomes a perfect gift when packaged by the hand of God. For whatever He does for us, *it shall be forever.*

To Jacob's fourteen years serving Laban, Laban added six more years for the sheep and cattle that Jacob acquired. During this time, Laban changed Jacob's wages ten times.

Then, after twenty years in Haran, Jacob began to see that Laban and his sons were becoming jealous of him and his possessions. They began to tighten their claims upon him and all his family.

In the flow of the Genesis account, God has been intimately near Jacob and all his household, dealing with them in predictable and caring ways. And, at this juncture, God was there with explicit instructions:

"Then the Lord said to Jacob, 'Return to the land of your fathers and to your kindred, and I will be with you". (Genesis 31:3)

At this very moment, Jacob realized he must leave with haste because he knew Laban would refuse to allow his daughters and their children to go away. Right now Laban was a distance from Haran, shearing his sheep. Jacob acted promptly with the consent and encouragement of both Leah and Rachael. Without delay, he and all his family and possessions fled from Haran and headed for the mountains of Gilead.

Laban did not know of their leaving until after three days. And then he went in hot pursuit, taking seven days to reach them. But God accosted Laban in the way and commanded him to leave Jacob and his family alone.

Confronting his angry Uncle, Jacob must meet the tense problem of reconciliation, and yet continue on his urgent mission to return to Canaan. At this time, it was imperative that they part company with Laban in peace.

With the help of God, in His counsel to Laban and also in His control over Jacob, giving him both courage and discretion, a pledge of understanding was established between them. A heap of stones became a boundary line over which neither was to cross to do harm. The word of their solemn agreement became known as the *Mizpah*

"May the Lord watch between you and me while we are absent one from another" (Gen. 31:49)

God was central in the healing of this relationship which closed with a benediction:

"The God of Abraham, the God of Nahor, and the God of their father judge between us. And Jacob swore by the Fear of his father Isaac.

Then Jacob offered a sacrifice on the mountain, and called his brethren to eat bread. And they ate bread and stayed all night on the mountain. And early in the morning Laban arose, and kissed his sons and daughters and blessed them. Then Laban departed and returned to his place." (Gen. 31: 53-55)

"So Jacob went on his way, and *the angels of God met him*." (Gen. 32: 1)

Here we observe a literary technique called an *inclusive*. When Jacob's departing Canaan was with the concourse of angels bearing gifts from the House of God, now as he returns to Canaan, "the angels met him there." The inclusive is often found in the Genesis narrative. It is like heaven's touch upon an earthly path imprinted with the steps of God as well as of man.

"When Jacob saw them, he said, 'This is God's camp!' And he called the place, Double camp, that is, Mahanaim."

In other words, I believe he is acknowledging that his two family groups belong to God. The family of

Leah which is followed in the order of their march, by the family of Rachael, are both belonging to God and to His high purposes for "the children of Jacob" which included by this time, eleven sons and one daughter.

They were a most vulnerable caravan plodding across foreign country, susceptible to the weathers, the untamed beasts of the forests or wilderness, and to the inhabitants of the land who could become inhospitable.

The greatest challenge yet was the imminent meeting with Esau again. But God drew their eyes toward His own providence, His angels met them. God's eye was upon them. His presence was in their midst.

Once more let us look into God's heart toward Jacob and his family:

"When you pass through the waters, I will be with you; and through the rivers, they shall not overflow you . . .

For I am the Lord your God, the Holy One of Israel, your Savior."

"Then Jacob sent messengers before him to Esau his brother in the land of Seir, the country of Edom. And he commanded them, saying, 'Speak thus to my lord, Esau, "Thus your servant Jacob says:" 'I have sojourned with Laban and stayed there until now. I have oxen, donkeys, flocks, and male and female servants, and I have sent to tell my lord that I might find favor in your sight.'" (Genesis 32:4,5)

When the messengers returned, they brought the news that Esau was coming to meet Jacob, and that he had four hundred men with him!

"So Jacob was greatly afraid and distressed, and he divided the people that were with him, and the flocks and herds and camels, into two companies. And he said, 'If Esau comes to the one company and attacks it, then the other company which is left will escape'." (Gen. 32 : 7,8)

At this time of keen alarm, we have the earnest prayer of Jacob to the One before Whom he walks. Perhaps it is the first actual prayer of Jacob recorded thus far in his biography, unless that vow made to God at Bethel could be understood as a prayer. The force of this supplication is Jacob's faith in God's own words of assurance to Him. This promise Jacob claims before the Lord as He calls on Him in his terror of facing Esau.

"O God of my father Abraham and God of my father Isaac, the Lord who said to me, 'Return to your country and to your kindred. And I will deal well with you.' I am not worthy of the least of all the mercies and of all the truth which You have shown Your servant; for I crossed over the Jordan with my staff; and now I have become two companies.

Deliver me, I pray, from the hand of Esau; for I fear him, lest he come and attack me and the mothers with the children. For You said, "I will surely treat you well, and make your descendants as the sand of the sea, which cannot be numbered for multitude." (Gen. 32: 9-12)

In the book of Hebrews chapter eleven, Jacob is listed among the heroes of faith by one sentence only. Yet it is a summary of his walk with God. It is his witness to the faithfulness of God as he blesses the two sons of Joseph near the close of his life just before being "gathered to his Fathers".

"By faith Jacob, when he was dying, blessed each of the sons of Joseph, and worshiped. *leaning* on the top of his staff." (Hebrews 11: 21) At this time Jacob testifies,

"God, before Whom my Fathers Abraham and Isaac walked, the God Who has fed me all my life long unto this day, *the Angel Who has redeemed me from all evil*, bless the lads . . ." (Gen. 48:15)

These words of Jacob allude to the next work of God
in Jacob's life at the time he is to face his brother Esau
beyond the ford of Jabbock en route to Canaan. It is
most certainly the climax in his spiritual walk with God,
a second life-changing meeting with God.

Jacob had just completed sending over the brook
his gifts to Esau to be received in three successive
stages, and then to follow next, his families in two
separate companies.

"He took them and sent them over the brook, and
sent over what he had.

Then Jacob was left alone."

Once Jacob was alone at Luz. And God met him,
and Jacob named that place *Bethel,* the House of God.

Again he is alone *"and a Man wrestled with him until
the breaking of day."*

This encounter with the Angel of the Lord the
scripture describes best:

"Now when He saw that He did not prevail against
him, He touched the socket of his hip; and the socket of
Jacob's hip was out of joint as He wrestled with him.
And He said,

'Let Me go for the day breaks!' But he said,
"I will not let You go unless You bless me!"

'So He said unto him,
"What is your name?" And he said,'
'Jacob'. "And He said,
'Your name shall no longer be called *Jacob,* but *Israel,
Prince with God ; for you have struggled with God and with
men, and have prevailed'.*

Then Jacob asked Him, saying "Tell me Your name,
I pray." And He said,
'Why is it that you ask about My name?'

And He blessed him there. And Jacob called the
name of the place Peniel.

"For I have seen God face to face, and my life is
preserved."

Just as he crossed over Penuel, the sun rose upon him, and he limped upon his hip." (Genesis 32:24-32)

Jacob, leaning on his staff, has now become a Prince with God. The secret of prevailing in faith, is that very paradox. The fact that he is *Jacob* requires that he cling to God. Jacob recognizes *he must lean on God*. When this is so, he finds, like Paul, that "when I am weak, then am I strong." Then he is Israel, not Jacob.

Faith is victory. Faith is bringing God into my life.

"Therefore most gladly I will rather boast in my infirmities that the power of Christ may rest upon me." (2Cor. 12:10)

Paul also speaks of fighting the good fight of faith

"I have fought the good fight. I have finished the race. I have kept the faith." (2 Timothy 4:7)

Israel, radiant with the Face of God in his reverie, crossed over the brook as the sun rose on him. He is limping but nevertheless Jacob is now Israel, a Prince with God.

He lifted up his eyes, and there Esau was coming, and with him were four hundred men.

Their meeting and reconciliation is one of the most beautiful scenes in Jacob's story. It begins:

"Esau ran to meet him, and embraced him, and fell on his neck and kissed him, and they wept."

Later Jacob begged Esau to receive his gifts to him, saying,

Then receive my present from my hand, inasmuch as I have seen your face *as* though *I had seen the face of God, and you were pleased with me.*"

*The favor of God* is what Jacob sees in his brother's face, now so changed. He recognizes this miracle as God's answer to his plea for mercy. In God's work upon Esau, Jacob sees once more the Face of God.

Peniel exemplifies victory. Jacob is no more *Jacob*. He is Israel who has found peace with his brother.

After awhile of fellowship together, the brothers parted to go their several ways, and Israel eventually settled in front of the city of Shechem. He bought the land upon which his tents were pitched there, and then erected an altar and called it *El Elohe Israel*, meaning, *God, the God of Israel. (Genesis 33:20)*

How long Jacob stayed near Shechem is not clear, but at this place Jacob suffered a severe trial with the behavior of his teenage sons and daughter, Dinah. This near disaster, resulted in God's immediate command:

"Arise, go up to Bethel and dwell there; and make an altar there to God who appeared to you when you fled from the face of Esau your brother." (Genesis 35:1)

Jacob's response was immediate. First he commanded his family and servants to put away all the foreign gods that were among them, and to purify themselves and change their garments. Jacob buried their idols under a terebinth tree at Shechem, and then said to them:

"Let us arise and go up to Bethel; and I will make an altar there to God, Who answered me in the day of my distress, and has been with me in the way that I have gone." (Genesis 35:3)

To travel at this time, was actually perilous for Israel. He had warned his sons that

"You have troubled me by making me obnoxious among the inhabitants in the land . . . . and since I am few in number, they will gather themselves together against me, and they shall kill me I shall be destroyed, my household and I". (Gen. 34:30)

But now in obedience to God's counsel, they "journeyed, and the terror of God was upon the cities that were all around them, and they did not pursue the sons of Jacob." (Gen. 35:5)

When Jacob returned to Bethel, it is significant that he called it *El Bethel*. He called it

"God of the House of God."

Central in his thinking is first God, and then the works of God. At Bethel, Jacob built an altar and worshiped Him. And here God talked again with Jacob, renewing all the Covenant promises to him.

It was at Bethel that God talked with Jacob a second time about his being no longer Jacob, but a Prince with God.

"Your name is Jacob; your name shall not be called Jacob anymore, but Israel shall be your name." (Gen. 35: 10)

In probing the significance of a new name given by God, George MacDonald leads us into an inspiring meditation on this subject:

"It is only when a man has *become* his name that God gives him the stone with his name upon it. Such a name cannot be given until the man *is the name.*" (From: George MacDonald, "An Anthology" by C S Lewis London Geoffrey Bles)

Jacob set up a pillar of stone at this site, and poured a drink offering and oil upon it to commemorate the place at Bethel where God talked with him again.

There had been sadness also at this second visit to Bethel. Rachael's nurse Deborah died and was buried under the terebinth tree which would be called "the terebinth of weeping."

More grief for Jacob would follow soon, for as they had left Bethel and were moving south toward Ephrath Jacob's beloved wife, Rachael, died as her second son, Benjamin was born. She had named him Ben Oni, son of sorrow, as she was dying, but his father named him Benjamin which means, "son of my right hand." At this place near Bethlehem, Jacob set up a marker called the Pillar of Rachael's Grave.

Jacob, now Israel, journeyed on to Hebron, and to Mamre where his father, Isaac, lived. It was the ancient home of Abraham where Isaac grew up. Jacob and Esau were both present when their father Isaac died, and "was gathered to his people" . . .

God keeps on shaping the destiny of His people. The wonder of Genesis is that although God's purposes concern the entire world, He is the Divine Companion of each individual who trusts in Him He is the God of Jacob, in His mercy; the God of Israel in His power. He yearns that all may trust in Him, and He is always the Rescue of each individual who chooses to seek Him with all his soul.

Shall we again let Isaiah state this truth?

"For the Lord has redeemed Jacob,
And glorified Himself in Israel." (Isaiah 44:22)

"The counsel of the Lord stands forever,
The plans of His heart to all generations.
From the place of His habitation He looks
On all the inhabitants of the earth;
He fashions their hearts *individually*
*He* considers all their works.
Behold the eye of the Lord is on those who fear Him,

On those who hope in His mercy,
To deliver their soul from death,
And to keep them alive in famine."
(Psalm 33: 11, 14,15, 18).

"The Lord is near to those who have a broken heart,
And saves such as have a contrite spirit."
(Psalm 34:18)

Israel and his twelve sons then settled in the valley of Hebron, and lived at the familiar site called Mamre when the story of Joseph, the firstborn son of Rachael begins.

Joseph whose name means *Increase* is key to a strategic new chapter in the history of the descendants of Israel. It begins a new Song, a new emphasis on the truth shown through all the pages of scripture, that

"If God be for us, who can stand against us?" (Romans 8:31)

In that "God was with Joseph", Joseph magnifies to us the heartening truth of the Sovereignty of God.

## Access

Prayer is the staircase from earth to heaven

To the throne room of the house of God.

Grace is found there, new mercies given,

Access to the Heart of God.

# Chapter Ten

## God is with Joseph

"But You, O Lord are a Shield for me, My
glory, and the One who lifts up my head."
(Psalm 3:3)

"Joseph, being seventeen years old was feeding the flock with his brothers". (Genesis 37:2)
Here begins a riveting short story, one of the finest in any literature just as it is presented in the Genesis record. The biography covers the last chapters of the book. (Genesis 37-50.)

The beginning scene that we find in the record of Joseph foreshadows the very wonderful ending of his story. The outstandingly handsome youth out in the field binding the sheaves along with his older brothers is markedly in contrast to them. He is wearing a beautiful tunic of rainbow colors. This cloak speaks of his special nearness to his father Jacob. Both Joseph and Jacob are grieving over the loss of Rachael who to Jacob was his chosen and beloved wife, and to Joseph, his own mother, and he, her firstborn son. Besides these bonds, there were deeper understandings in their love for one another. Joseph revered his father's standards of life. He had profound reverence for God, and could never tire of hearing all that his father could tell him of God's caring for his grandfather Isaac, and of his great grandfather Abraham. He held sacred the Covenant God had made with his Fathers, and kept in his heart the quiet assurance of the Divine destiny of his people. For this reason, some of the conversation and ungodly behavior of a few of his older half-brothers became a concern to him. And he reported their behavior to his father. Joseph had confided in his father hoping that the problem might be corrected. However Joseph seemed unaware that these attitudes were building envy and hatred toward him in the hearts of his brothers. Adding to this resentment toward him, Joseph had naively shared two dreams he could not resist telling to his brothers and to his father. The dreams were mysteries to him, but they so impressed him that he could not keep them to himself. He told them:

"There we were binding sheaves in the field. Then, behold my sheaf arose and also stood upright; and indeed your sheaves stood all around and bowed down to my sheaf." (Genesis 37:7)

His siblings responded with the scornful query,

"Shall you indeed reign over us?"

But Joseph seemed not to perceive the emotion stirring in their hearts, and in youthful indiscretion, he proceeded to tell his second vivid dream. With wonder, he exclaimed,

"Look, I have dreamed another dream. And this time the eleven stars and the sun and the moon bowed down to me." (Genesis37:9)

As he related these dreams, I believe Joseph was as puzzled as his parents and brothers. This time, his father also rebuked his young son: "What is this dream that you have dreamed? Shall your mother (Leah) and I and your brothers indeed come to bow down to the earth before you?" (Gen.37:10)

Then we read this significant statement, "And his brothers envied him, *but his father kept the matter in mind.*" (Genesis 37:11)

Thus at the beginning of his story, we have Joseph in his coat of many colors and his two singular dreams. This beginning foreshadows the conclusion. His story is to close with Joseph the exalted Ruler in Egypt, second only to Pharaoh himself, dispensing bread to the famine stricken people from far and near. And one day among them will appear ten Hebrew shepherds, his very same brothers, bowing before him beseeching relief. The Ruler of Egypt in his royal attire and Egyptian speech will recognize his brothers and remember those dreams. Recalling the fields and their labors together, Joseph remembers his father and their final embrace as he left to find his brothers, never imagining he would not see that valley of Hebron for another more than forty years. Deeply moved, yet restraining his emotions in front of his siblings, He thinks of how the dreams of his youth have come to pass as Joseph's true story reaches its glorious conclusion.

All that has come between this opening and closing of the Genesis account of Joseph describes God's sovereign ordering of events working out His divine purposes in every changing circumstance both fortunate and unfortunate. It is an in depth study of the consoling truth emphasized throughout the scriptures, that God is in control *always*, working out His redemptive purposes with power and grace. A truth often quoted by Mrs. Howard Taylor in her biography of Hudson Taylor of China, is demonstrated clearly in Joseph's life.

"Ill God blesses is our good, and unblessed good is ill
And that is right which seems most wrong if it be His sweet will."

This is the same fact expressed in the epistle to the Romans.

"And we know that all things work together for good to those who love God, to those who are called according to His purpose." (Romans 8:28)

Also, in the ending of his story, Joseph, assuring his brothers of full forgiveness, says to them:

"But as for you, you meant evil against me, but God meant it for good in order to bring it about as it is today, to save many people alive. Now therefore do not be afraid." (Genesis 50:20)

Back to the beginning of the story, at their home in Hebron, Joseph's father speaks to his son.

"Are not your brothers feeding the flock in Shechem?" Behind these words is the strong implication of peril. The brothers had made enemies in Shechem in the matter of Dinah, their sister, and Israel was concerned about their welfare.

"Come, I will send you to them." So Joseph said to him,

"Here I am."

"So Israel said to him: 'Please go and see if it is well with your brothers and well with the flocks, and bring back word to me.'" (Genesis 37:13,14)

Without any qualms, Joseph set out to find his brothers. He found them not at Shechem, but was told there that his brothers had gone on to Dothan where Joseph saw them at a distance and hastened to meet them with joy.

"Now when they saw him afar off, even before he came near them, they conspired against him to kill him. Then they said to one another,

'Come therefore, let us now kill him and cast him into some pit, and we shall say "Some wild beast has devoured him." We shall see what will become of his dreams.' (Genesis 37:20)

"And Reuben said to them, 'Shed no blood, but cast him into this pit which is in the wilderness, and do not lay a hand on him'—that he might deliver him out of their hands and bring him back to his father."

"Then they took him and cast him into a pit. And the pit was empty. There was no water in it.

And then they sat down to eat a meal. Then they lifted up their eyes and looked, and there was a company of Ishmaelites coming from Gilead with their camels bearing spices, balm, and myrrh, on their way to carry them down to Egypt." (Genesis 37:22-25)

At this point Judah spoke up to persuade the others not to kill their brother, but rather, to sell him to the Ishmaelites who were even then passing by.

"Let not our hand be upon him, for he is our brother and our flesh. And the brothers listened to Judah, and pulled up Joseph and lifted him from the pit. They promptly sold him to the Ishmaelites for 20 shekels of silver.

"And they took Joseph to Egypt." (Genesis 37: 28)

By the time Reuben returned, he found the pit was empty, and Joseph was gone. His prayers, and Joseph's anguished supplications had not been granted. Why?

They could not have imagined that God was programming a far better future for Israel and his children. One that would be "exceeding abundantly above all" they could ask or think! Ephesians 3:20)

Yet the tragedy of this event would deepen, as we read of how the brothers soaked Joseph's tunic in the blood of a goat, and took it to their aged father.

"Without doubt, Joseph is torn to pieces", Jacob mourned. Binding sackcloth around his waste, Israel would not be comforted,

'For I shall go down to the grave to my son in mourning' Thus Israel wept for him." (Genesis 37:35)

We can imagine the trauma Joseph felt, and the unmitigated grief and suffering Joseph experienced as he thought of his father, and as he faced the unknown in a strange land.

Would he be able to survive the strain? What would he do? What would happen to him next? We have a clear answer to these questions in the words that recur throughout his trials beginning at this time and continuing through the years to come. *"But* God *was with Joseph"*. It is this fact that makes all the difference between loss and gain; between despair and spiritual resources bringing the blessings of heaven. The text reads, *"But God was with Joseph."*

The Psalmist speaks of hiding in "the secret of His Presence." And here is the gist of Joseph's faith in his walk with God. (Psalm 31:20)

Following the changeful and contrasting circumstances of his life in Egypt, this is the note repeated like the drumbeat of victory, *"But God was with Joseph"*

Just here I would like to quote lines from the writings of George MacDonald again:

"Do not think of God only as being always over our heads, merely throwing over us a widespread benevolence. Can you imagine the tenderness of a mother's heart, taking her child to soothe and minister to it. That is like God. That is God. It is God's way.

His hand is not only over us, but recollect what David said,: 'His hand was upon me . . . . wherever I go, God is there—beneath me, before me, His hand is upon me: if I go to sleep, He is there; when I go down to the dead, He is there.'"

And he continues to write,

"Everywhere is God. The earth beneath us is His hand upholding us; the waters are in the hollow of it. Every spring-fountain of gladness about us is His making and His delight. He tends us and cares for us; He is close to us, breathing into our nostrils the breath of life, and breathing into our spirit this thought and that thought to make us look up and realize the love and care around us." (from "Discovering the Character of God")

This fact of God's presence with him proved to be of his inner adequacy and poise in the life of Joseph. At every turning point, whether apparently good or apparently bad, this word, "God was with Joseph," unveils how Joseph could hide his sackcloth of sorrows and personal loss, to wear instead a "garment of praise".

Standing on the slave block in Egypt, the Hebrew youth is calm and self-controlled because he is more keenly aware of God's presence than all the noise around him.

And in the next comments about Joseph, we find that he has matured. He is referred to as a *man*. Now owned by the Egyptian named Potiphar, "an officer of Pharaoh, captain of the guard." (Genesis 39:1)

It became obvious to those around him, that Joseph possessed inward strength of mind and soul in a most unusual degree. *"The Lord was with Joseph*, and he was a successful man, and he was in the house of his master the Egyptian. And his master saw that the Lord was with him, and that the Lord made all he did to prosper in his hand.

So Joseph found favor in his sight, and served him. Then he made him overseer of his house, and all that he had he put in his hand." (Genesis 39:4)

In a short while, Potiphar had put Joseph in total charge of all his household. And the Egyptian master realized that the Lord was blessing life in all things because of Joseph.

At this time, Joseph would learn the Egyptian language as it was spoken at the top level of society. He would acquire the culture of the Egyptians, who, by the way, looked down on shepherds. Yet Joseph, a Hebrew highly esteemed, "was handsome in form and appearance." And his master, Potiphar trusted Joseph and discerned his intelligence and character.

How many years had passed in the elegant household of Potiphar is not known. It may have been five or six. But suddenly an unfortunate incident changed everything once more for Joseph.

The wife of Potiphar one day tried to seduce Joseph at a time when no one was around. But Joseph recoiled from her, leaving his cloak with her as she had torn it from him. He fled, but was defenseless when she used his mantle to support her story to her husband.

To Joseph the thought of such sin was intolerable. He could not dishonor his master, and more important, he would not sin against God.

"To such a heart, sin is disgusting. It sees a thing as it is, that is, as God sees it" (MacDonald, Discovering the Character of God p 262)

Joseph was innocent of wrongdoing, but unable to defend himself against the slander of Potiphar's wife.

To his amazement and shock, Joseph suddenly found himself in the King's notoriously miserable Dungeon. He was with felons accused of crimes, out of favor with Pharaoh, or with the captain of the guard. Again, Joseph has been brought low. We read, *"He was there in prison."* But once more his faith would triumph over despair. For at this formidable turning in the road the theme line sounds forth again,

*"But the Lord was with Joseph* and showed him mercy, and He gave him favor in the sight of the keeper of the prison. And the keeper of the prison committed to Joseph's hand all the prisoners who were in the prison, whatever they did there, it was his doing. The keeper of the prison did not look into anything that was under Joseph's hand, because the Lord was with him; and whatever he did, the Lord made it to prosper." (Genesis 39:21-23)

This again is the divine difference between misery and contentment. The prison remained cold and bleak. Yet Joseph thought about the act that Potipher could have had him killed. Mercifully his life was spared. Perhaps Potiphar had not believed his wife's story after all.

Nevertheless Joseph was there in prison. Tomorrow would dawn as yesterday. The same routines, the same absence of the daylight outside, the gloom would remain. Dank walls of the dungeon seemed to ward off hope. Life seemed purposeless. *Yet* God *was with Joseph*.

God is "the God of Hope." With Him there is no dead end. In prison, Joseph would continue to live in God's presence, appropriate His peace and joy, and fulfill his responsibilities in serving God as well as his fellow prisoners.

Then one day something unusual happened. The captain of the guard charged Joseph with the care of two officers of Pharaoh whom he had sent to prison. They were the king's butler and his baker. Now Joseph was responsible for their well being while they were in the prison.

"And Joseph came in to the men in the morning and looked at them, and saw that they were sad." In talking with them he found out why they were troubled. Each had dreamed a dream they could not understand. "And there is no interpreter of it." they told him.

"Do not interpretations belong to God?" Joseph asked. Tell them to me."

As they related their dreams to Joseph, God gave him the interpretation of them. Each prediction came to pass. The baker was hanged, but the butler was restored to his office as the Cupbearer to Pharaoh. (Genesis 40)

This incident gave Joseph a straw of hope. Could the chief butler then speak a good word for him to Pharaoh? And Joseph asked a favor of him.

"Make mention of me unto Pharaoh, and get me out of this house." Joseph's request was reasonable.

"For indeed I was stolen away from the land of the Hebrews, and also I have done nothing here that they should put me into the dungeon."

And the chief butler gladly promised Joseph that he would do this. "Yet the chief butler did not remember Joseph, but forgot him." (Genesis40:23)

What would have happened if he had remembered Joseph at this time? Surely it would have been "unblessed good". God's greater purpose for Joseph would have been foiled. Undoubtedly Joseph would have made his way back to Hebron. But God in love and mercy did not grant Joseph's request. Joseph waited, hoping each day for a messenger from the King releasing him. But he must wait for two more full years.

How Joseph would later thank the Lord for unanswered prayers! The timing would not have been right. Both Egypt and Israel with his family would have missed the deliverance from famine throughout the land, and much more important, the increase of Israel in developing into a great nation could not have come to pass.

So often our perspective is nearsighted and off course in the eyes of the Lord. But His sovereign will in every detail works for us "unto the praise of the glory of His Grace". (Ephesians 1:12)

In the tests of longsuffering and waiting days and months and even years, we can know His blessing only as we pray, "Not my will, but Thine be done." (Luke 22:42)

But at last, when Joseph was now thirty years of age, God's time for Joseph had come! We have a most insightful summary of the hand of God upon Joseph in Psalms 105:16-2

"Moreover He called for a famine in the land
He destroyed all the provision of bread.
He sent a *man* before them—
Joseph—who was sold as a slave.
They hurt his feet with fetters,
He was laid in irons.

Until the time that his word came to pass,
The word of the Lord tested him.
The king sent and released him,
The ruler of the people let him go free.
And ruler of all of his possessions."

It came to pass that Pharaoh had two troubling dreams that none of his magi could interpret. Then the chief butler at last remembered Joseph and told the King all about the Hebrew young man who was blessed of God with ability to correctly interpret dreams.

"Then Pharaoh sent and called Joseph, and they brought him hastily out of the dungeon; and he shaved changed his clothing and came to Pharaoh." (Gen. 41:14) Here Joseph before Pharaoh does not hesitate to acknowledge God. When Pharaoh said to Joseph,

"I have heard it said of you that you can understand a dream to interpret it." Joseph replied,

"It is not in me. God will give Pharaoh an answer of peace."

After Pharaoh told Joseph his two dreams about seven fat cows swallowed up by seven lean ones, yet remaining lean, and of seven full heads of grain consumed by seven withered ones, Joseph answered him with clarity and assurance:

"The dreams are one. God has shown Pharaoh what He is about to do. And the dream was repeated to Pharaoh twice because the thing is established by God, and God will shortly bring it to pass."(Gen. 41:32)

Joseph told Pharaoh that seven years of great plenty would come, but they would be followed by seven years of most severe famine throughout the land. It would be a famine that would so deplete the land that the seven years of plenty would be forgotten as though they never were.

Then Joseph continued, caught up in the urgency for orderly preparation for those famine years. He spoke with amazing understanding and fervor advising the King on how to save Egypt from desolation during those years of great want and distress.

As Joseph spoke, Pharaoh understood at once what he must do. "And Pharaoh said to his servants,

'Can we find such a one as this, a man in whom is the Spirit of God?"

"Then Pharaoh said to Joseph, 'Since God has shown you all this, there is no one so discerning and wise as you You shall be over my house, and all my people shall be ruled according to your word; only in regard to the throne will I be greater than you.

See, I have set you over all he land of Egypt'.

Then Pharaoh took his signet ring off his hand and put it on Joseph's hand; and he clothed him in garments of fine linen and put a gold chain around his neck. And he had him ride in the second chariot which he had; and they cried out before him,

'Bow the knee!'

So he set him over the whole land of Egypt." (Gen. 41:41-43)

Pharaoh gave Joseph a name, Zaphnath-Paaneah, and the name meaning, *God speaks and He lives* is in itself a statement about the God who is with Joseph.

He was given as a wife, Asenath, the daughter of the Priest of On. And throughout the years of abundance, Joseph went out over the whole land of Egypt garnering into huge store houses much grain, "as the sand of the sea", and built store houses for food in every city in the land.

During the years of plenty, two sons were born to Joseph. The firstborn Joseph named *Manasseh*: "For God has made me to forget all my toil and all my father's house"

And he named the second son *Ephraim*: "For God has caused me to be fruitful in the land of my affliction,"

With the coming of the famine years, God brings about the culmination of His purpose in sending Joseph to Egypt. In heightening dramatic suspense, and incredible perfection in every detail, the family of Joseph becomes united in the awesome presence of Joseph, the one who was "separate from his brothers."

Through the more than twenty years that Israel mourned for the son who "was not", the hearts of the brothers have changed and mellowed in remorse and in repentance for their guilt. Benjamin is found again by his brother, Joseph. Judah and Simeon have been capable of heroic speeches, eloquent in loyalty and love. Israel is wonderfully comforted, and witnesses his faith in the God

"Who has fed me all my life until now . . . and has redeemed me from all evil." (Genesis 48:15)

Joseph tested his brothers, but proved them wholly changed, and extended to them his complete forgiveness, promising to take care of them.

The crescendo sweeping up into the climax of the story increases with Pharaoh's welcome to the Hebrew shepherds, the family of Joseph. The King gives them the finest area of their country, the Land of Goshen.

God has brought to pass the prophecy spoken to
Abraham which said his people would sojourn in Egypt
until they became a multitude to bear the Name of the
living God before all the nations of the world. Realizing
this prophecy would mean for the children of Israel
another 400 years in Egypt, Joseph arranged for the
future that his bones be carried back to Canaan at the
time the nation would return.

Right through to the poetic ending of Genesis when
Jacob blesses all his sons, he includes both sons of
Joseph to be heads of their tribe, thus giving the double
portion to his most eminent son, Joseph.


Joseph's words to his brothers highlight the truth of
*God in* control. Not only is He sovereign, but He never
walks away from the one who has chosen to walk with Him.

And Joseph assured the brothers who sold him into
Egypt, that

"God sent me before you to preserve a posterity for
you in the earth, and to save your lives by a great
deliverance. So now, it was not you who sent me here
but God." (Genesis 48: 8)

Also over in Beer Sheba, in contemplating Egypt,
Israel was reassured by God Who never failed to guide
him at every turning in his pilgrimage. At this time he
knew that Joseph was alive, and the Ruler in Egypt.
Israel had decided to go and see his son in Egypt, but
he first went to Beer Sheba to offer sacrifices to God.

"And God spoke to Israel in the visions of the night,
and said, 'Jacob, Jacob!' And he said, 'Here am I'. And
He said,

'I am God, the God of your father. Do not fear to go
down into Egypt, for I will make of you a great nation
there. I will go down with you to Egypt, and I will surely
bring you up again. (Genesis 46: 2,3)

The words closing the Genesis documentary of Joseph, and, in fact, the book of Genesis as well, focus our thoughts again on the God of Joseph, the ever-present God.

"But as for you, you meant evil against me; but God meant it for good . . . to save many people alive." (Genesis 50: 20)

Israel lived in Egypt with his increasing family for seventeen more years. And just before he died, he spoke prophetically to each of his sons. It would be that from the tribe of Judah that Shiloh would come. Shiloh is a title of Messiah, the Coming One, the Christ. With Israel's final tribute to Joseph, these beautiful words bring to a close Joseph's most excellent story. (Genesis 49: 22-26)

> Joseph is a fruitful bough
> A fruitful bough by a well;
>
> The archers have bitterly grieved him,
> Shot at him and hated him.
> But his bow remained in strength,
> And the arms of his hands were made strong
> By the hands of the Mighty God of Jacob
> (From there is the Shepherd, the Stone of Israel),
> By the God of your father Who will help you,
> And the Almighty Who will bless you
> With the blessings of heaven above,
> Blessings of the deep that lies beneath, . . .
> Up to the utmost bounds of the everlasting hills.
> They shall be on the head of Joseph,
> And on the crown of the head of him
> who was separate from his brothers.

We think of One "crowned with glory and honor" Who is yet to reign over the nations, and we remember

His Name which is "God with us", Immanuel. And, like Joseph, we find that Name to be our "strong Tower" which we may run into and find safety no matter what "archers bitterly grieve."

God with us can only mean those unfailing blessings of El Shaddai, the Almighty. His presence brings "the blessings of heaven above, of the deep beneath, up to the utmost bounds of the everlasting hills." Like Joseph, we too may know that promise, "I will never leave you or forsake you." (Hebrews 13:5)

These close-up views of persons who walked with God, help us to realize that God is the God of the individual. His eternal purposes are vast, and have garnered to His Kingdom through the ages the "multitude which no man can number."

Yet we find Him dealing with you and me on a one on one level.


Here I would like to continue with George MacDonald's soliloquy on this theme, he says,

"Not only then has each man his individual relation to God, but each man has his peculiar relation to God. He is to God, made after his own fashion, and that of no one else. Hence he can worship God as no one else can worship Him. With every man God has a secret, the secret of a new name. In every man there is a loneliness, an inner chamber of peculiar life to which God only can enter.

(George MacDonald "An Anthology" by C S Lewis, London Geoffrey Bles

Of course the general term, man, means a person, and the truth emphasized is the wonder of God's impartial complete attention to the *one* person. One knows no limitation in His understanding love and mercy. The individual differs from another widely. But

God relates to each one individually. And the individual's audience with God is never interrupted or cut short by any other's. God is nearer to each one who loves Him, nearer than his own consciousness of self. May it be true to say of us also that they walked with God."

# Trinity of Love

O Son of God, Eternal Word of
Eternal Father given,
Eternal Spirit shown,
Immanuel, Thou Lamb of God
For our redemption slain
Forbidding Death it's victory,
Now risen from the grave.
Immutable redemption claimed
In riches of Thy grace
To make us Thine inheritance
From every tongue and race

A train the length of time proceeds
Unto Thine open Door
Inviting us to dwell with Thee
To live where Thou art Home.
And in Thy likeness stand before Thee
In righteousness Thine own
To serve Thee as Thine angels do
Beholding there Thy face
Upon Thy changeless mercy stayed,
Thou God of Ancient Days
Thou Trinity of Love.

# Epilogue

They walked with God, these eight individuals who lived in the age when no written scriptures existed. The Patriarchs of the Book of Beginnings knew God as He revealed Himself to them from time to time. They heard "the voice of His word". The voice of a person conveys so much more of who that person is than any written words can do. And their response to that present Being Who made Himself known to them at every turn, set them in the way of His footsteps. They walked with God by faith. In faith they "heeded the voice of His word". And this they are doing today in that Kingdom existing now in heaven. There the angels, along with all the redeemed whom He calls His own children, continue heeding the voice of His word.

"Bless the Lord, all you hosts, you ministers (servants) of His who do His pleasure." (Psalm 103 : 20-21)

I have found much blessing in concentrating upon the interior biography, of each of these eight outstanding characters, not just the narrative of their outward story and experiences. It is their inward story, and their growing knowledge and understanding of the living God that has revealed God Himself to me with deeper insight. It has come to me with inspiring conviction that He is indeed the *same Person* we see in the full noonday light of the Gospels.

Jesus opened a glorious window for us upon that kingdom in heaven. Speaking to leaders in Israel, He tells us how that God is the God of the living. He *is* the God of Abraham, Isaac and Jacob. For they live, being beyond the possibility of death anymore, but now as "the sons of the Resurrection," they are like the angels, yet better than they since they are called the "sons of God." (Luke 21: 34-38)

This glimpse into Heaven is only one of many that the Lord gives us in the New Testament which is obviously the continuation of the Old Testament. Each new insight in knowing truth as it is in Christ, reveals the same Person the Patriarchs knew as they walked with God united to Him by faith.

When Christ mourned over Jerusalem, He said,

"How often I wanted to gather your children together, but you were not willing . . ." (Matt. 23:37)

He was only thirty-two years of age then, yet here, once more, Christ is speaking from another dimension, for He is that One "Whose goings forth have been of old, even from everlasting." (Micah 5:2).

He is the very Person Who is revealed to individuals of the Beginnings. His saving love was the same to all who responded to Him in trust and obedience although they lived on earth in the first millenniums of human history. In awe of Him, we listen as the Christ of God says to the rulers of His people,

"Before Abraham was, *I Am.*" (John 8:58)

The more Abraham's inner life with God unfolds, the more we find "the God of Glory" that Abraham knew, is also the One Paul speaks of in his prayer for the Ephesians that

"The Father of Glory may give to you the spirit of wisdom and *revelation* in the knowledge of Him." (Acts 7:1 & Ephesians 1:17)

Being in awe of the Reality of God begins that wisdom so necessary to the inner person we are. And on that holy ground, knowing that God IS, we discover for ourselves "the voice of His word" addressing us. We therefore can make the choice which transforms our lives as it has for every person who wills to say *Yes* to Him.

I have heard "Old age is not for sissies". This is so, I'm sure. But I believe it is true for every stage of life that we cannot walk alone and make it. Yet we need not. In fact, it is God Himself in all the wonder of His completeness, the Father, the Son, and the Holy Spirit, Who desires that each of us, find in Him salvation and peace.

With the conviction that God is available to us no matter what our exterior circumstances may be, makes all the difference in our lives. God met the Fathers where they were in their own setting and generation, and dealt with them according to His will and character. Let the Beginnings also teach us this.

We thank God for these eight Portraits of Faith in the time scope of Genesis because they found God in reality. They knew Him personally. In knowing Him, they chose to live in His presence, and to walk with Him.

In obedience motivated by love, *they walked with God.*

# Notes on the Quotations

## INTRODUCTION

1. Genesis 1:1
2. "George MacDonald, An Anthology" by C.S. Lewis, London, Geoffrey Bles, page 116 #321.
3. Sidlow Baxter, GOD SO LOVED
4. 2 Cor. 2:16

## CHAPTER ONE (A.W.Tozer)

1. Psalm 8:3, 4
2. Genesis 2:7
3. Ecc. 3:10
4. Hebrews 12:9
5. Genesis 1:28
6. Psalm 8:6
7. John 1:1-4
8. A. W. Tozer, THE CHRISTIAN BOOK OF MYSTIC VERSE by Jeanne Marie De La Motte-Guyon, "I Love My God", page 65, top.
9. Job 36:22
10. C.S. Lewis from Reflections on the Psalms, Chapter 9
11. The Westminster Catechism . . . Man's Chief End, etc.
12. A. W. Tozer THE CHRISTIAN BOOK OF MYSTIC VERSE "The Celestial Country" by Bernard of Cluny, page 140 last stanza.

13. A. W. Tozer THE CHRISTIAN BOOK OF MYSTIC VERSE "O Jesus Most Wonderful"by Bernard of Clairvaux, page 95.
14. 2 Cor. 5:4
15. 2 Peter 3:9

## CHAPTER TWO (Psalm 51:11)

1. Isaiah 43:1
2. A. W. Tozer, THE PURSUIT OF GOD, page 33.
3. A. W. Tozer, THE PURSUIT OF GOD, page 34.
4. A. W. Tozer, THE CHRISTIAN BOOK OF MYSTIC VERSE, by F. W. Faber,"The Eternal Father", page 20.
5. A. W. Tozer, THE PURSUIT OF GOD, Chapter 6, The Speaking Voice.
6. F. B. Meyer, THE WAY INTO THE HOLIEST
7. Prov. 14:12
8. Genesis 3:3
9. Matthew 4:10
10. James 4:7-8
11. Matthew 4:11
12. I Cor. 10:13
13. Matthew 4:4
14. Isaiah 53:3
15. I Peter 2:24
16. Romans 3:23
17. Hebrews 9:25
18. Genesis 3:23
19. Genesis 3:19

    George MacDonald "Discovering the Character ofGod" page 259, by Michael Phillips, Bethany House Publishers
20. Psalm 100:5
21. Genesis 3:15
22. Hymn "Alas, And Did My Savior Bleed" by Isaac Watts, stanza Three

23. Sidlow Baxter in "God So Loved"
24. Luke 18:29,30
25. John 3:16
26. Romans 6:4

## CHAPTER THREE (Proverbs 16:6)

1. Genesis 4:1-16
2. Genesis 4:1
3. Genesis 3:15
4. C. S. Lewis, "the everyday-ness of life is penetrated by glory".
5. I Peter 3:4
6. Fredk A. Filby, "The Lord Weighs the Heart" (Prov. 21:2b)
7. George MacDonald "Discovering the Character of God"
8. George MacDonald "Discovering the Character of God", Page 51
9. Genesis 4:3, 4
10. Hebrews 12:1
11. I Peter 1:20
12. Hebrews 11:4
13. Genesis 4:7
14. II Peter 3:9
15. James 1:14-15
16. Hebrews 12:22-24
17. Proverbs 12:28
18. A. W. Tozer, THE CHRISTIAN BOOK OF MYSTIC VERSE, from "At the Lord's Table" by Horatius Bonar, page 108, stanza 6. (Christian Publications, Camp Hill, PA).

## CHAPTER FOUR (Matthew 24:42)

1. George MacDonald, "The Character of God" by Michael R. Phillips, Bethany House Publishers

2. Ravi Zechariah, "Cries of the Heart"
3. Jude 15
4. Jude 14
5. Rev. 21:25
6  Psalm 25:14
7. An old hymn "Eternity with all its years . . . ."
8. Brother Lawrence "Practicing the Presence of God".
9. "Twentieth Century Testimony" by Thomas Howard from Malcolm Muggeridge.
10. Hebrews 11:4
11. A. W. Tozer THE CHRISTIAN BOOK OF MYSTIC VERSE, "The Celestial Country" by Bernard of Cluny, page 133, top.
12. Titus 2:13
13. I Cor. 15:51, 52
14. I Thess. 4:17
15. John 14:3
16. 2 Cor. 5:8
17. Psalm 23:3
18. Eph. 1:6
19. Hebrews 11:6

## CHAPTER FIVE (Psalm 9:10)

1. Genesis 6:5
2. Genesis 6:3
3. Genesis 5:29
4. Genesis 8:21
5. Genesis 6:12, 13
6. George MacDonald, "The Character of God", page 194, by Michael Phillips, Bethany House, Minneapolis, Minn.
7. Genesis 6:13-15
8. Genesis 6:18
9. Hebrews 11:7

10. Genesis 6:22
11. Matt. 11:28
12. Epistle of Barnabas (120 ad) from "Faith Under Fire", day 69 by David Winters, Harold Shaw Publishers, Wheaton, Ill.
13. Genesis 7:1
14. Genesis 7:4
15. Genesis 7:16
16. Psalm 46:10
17. A. W. Tozer THE CHRISTIAN BOOK OF MYSTIC VERSE, "The Greatness of God" by F. W. Faber, page 14,. Christian Publications, Camp Hill, PA
18. Psalm 32:7
19. Genesis 7:24
20. Jer. 29:11-13
21. Wesley L. Ducarel "The highest expression of faith, etc."
22. Psalm 43:4
23. A.W.Tozer "As God dwells in your thoughts . . ."
24. Ravi Zecharias, "Cries of the Heart", "Worship is the supreme expression in life . . .".
25. Genesis 9:11
26. Genesis 9:6
27. Rev. 7:9

## CHAPTER SIX (Job 28:28)

1. George MacDonald "Discovering the Character of God"
2. Psalm 103:19
3. Psalm 103:20, 21
4. Ezekiel 14:15, 20
5. James 5:11
6. Job 1:3
7. Rev. 22:4
8. Job 1:8, 2:5

9.  Job 28:20, 28
10. Frederick W. Faber, "There is a Wideness in God's Mercy" (hymn)
11. Job 1:20
12. Job 1:21
13. Job 2:7
14. Job 2:8
15. Job 2:10
16. Job 2:11
17. Job 38:7
18. Job 13:14-16
19. Job 19:21-27
20. Job 23:3
21. Job 23:8-10
22. George MacDonald "Discovering the Character of God", Page 179
23. Job 31:40
24. Job 35:10
25. Job 32:12
26. Job 36:22
27. Job 37:14
28  Job 37:32
29. Job 38:3
30. Job 9:32
31. Job 38:4, 7, 12
32. Job 38:36
33. Job 42:5, 6
34. Job 42:2
35. St. Augustine from "The Legacy of Sovereign Joy", John Piper, Crossway Books,Wheaton, Ill.

## CHAPTER SEVEN (John 8:56)

1.  2 Chron. 20:8
2.  James 2:23
3.  Genesis 17:1

4. Genesis 12:1-3
5. Isaiah 41:13
6. Genesis 12:6
7. Genesis 12:7
8. Genesis 14:19, 20
9. Genesis 14: 22, 23
10. Genesis 17
11. Genesis 15
12. Dr. Robertson McQuilkin from the summer issue of Connection, CIU 2001.
13. Galatians 3:8, 16
14. Hebrews 11:10
15. Genesis 23:6
16. Romans 4:18-21
17. Genesis 17
18. Genesis 18:9, 10
19. Genesis 18:14
20. Charles Wesley, "Faith Mighty Faith"
21. Hebrews 11:11
22. John 8:56
23. John 8:58
24. Micah 5:2
25. John 3:16
26. John 1:14
27. Luke24:27

# CHAPTER EIGHT (George MacDonald)

1. Genesis 21:33
2. Genesis 22:1, 2
3. Luke 22:42
4. Genesis 22:3, 4
5. Genesis 22:5
6. Genesis 22:7, 8
7. Genesis 22:11, 12
8. Genesis 22:14

9. Genesis 22:15-17
10. Hebrews 11:17-19
11. Job 27:19
12. Matt.22:29-32; Mark 12:24-27; Luke 20:34-38
13. Hebrews 11:13, 16
14. Malcolm Muggeridge, Twentieth Century Testimony, by Thomas Howard, Thomas Nelson Press.
15. Genesis 24:27
16. Genesis 25:21
17. Genesis 26:11-33
18. Genesis 26:14
19. Genesis 26:16
20. George Buttrick-1895-1980 from Devotional Classics, edited by John Foster and James Bryan Smith, Hoddard and Stoughton, London.
21. George MacDonald "Discovering the Character of God", Page 129
22. Genesis 26:22
23. Genesis 26:24, 25
24. Genesis 26:27-33
25. Psalm 34:5
26. Isaiah 26:3, 4

## CHAPTER NINE (Rev. 3:29)

1. Matthew 5:1
2. Genesis 28:13
3. Genesis 28:15, 16
4. Genesis 28: 15-17
5. Psalm 46:7
6. Malcolm Muggeridge, Twentieth Century Testimony, by Thomas Howard, Thomas Nelson Press.
7. Genesis 28:21
8. Genesis 28:22
9. Isaiah 41:8-10,13

11. John 1:47-51
12. Prov. 3:5,6
13. Isaiah 43:1
14. Genesis 29:30
15. Galatians 6:7
16. Hosea 8:7
17. Psalm 23:3
18. Genesis 31:3
19. Genesis 31:49
20. Genesis 31:53-55
21. Genesis 32:1
22. Genesis 32:4, 5
23. Genesis 32:7, 8
24. Genesis 32:9-12
25. Hebrews 11:21
26. Genesis 48:15
27. Genesis 32:24-32
28. 2 Cor. 12:10
29. 2 Timothy 4:7
30. Genesis 33:20
31. Genesis 35:1
32. Genesis 35:3
33. Genesis 34:30
34. Genesis 35:5
35. Genesis 35:10
36. George MacDonald "An Anthology" by C.S. Lewis, London, Geoffrey Bles
37. Isaiah 44:22
38. Psalm 33:11, 14, 15, 18
39. Psalm 34:18
40. Romans 8:31

# CHAPTER TEN (Psalm 3:3)

1. Genesis 37:2
2. Genesis 37-50
3. Genesis 37:7

4. Genesis 37:9
5. Genesis 37:10
6. Genesis 37:11
7. Mrs. Howard Taylor, from her biography of Hudson Taylor of China. "Ill God blesses is our good . . ."
8. Romans 8:28
9. Genesis 50:20
10. Genesis 37:13, 14
11. Genesis 37:20
12. Genesis 37:22-25
13. Genesis 37:28
14. Ephesians 3:20
15. Genesis 37:35
16. Psalm 31:20
17. Genesis 39:1
18. Genesis 39:4
19. Genesis 39:21-23
20. Genesis 40:23
21. Ephesians 1:12
22. Luke 22:42
23. Psalm 105:16-22
24. Genesis 41:14
25. Genesis 41:32
26. Genesis 41:41-43
27. Genesis 48:15
28. Genesis 48:8
29. Genesis 46:2, 3
30. Genesis 50:20
31. Genesis 49:22-26
32. Hebrews 13:5
33. George MacDonald "An Anthology" by C.S. Lewis, London, Geoffrey Bles

# EPILOGUE

1. Psalm 103:20, 21
2. Luke 21:34-38
3. Matt. 23:37
4. Micah 5:2
5. John 8:58
6. Acts 7:1 and Eph. 1:17